PASSOVER COOKERY
In the Kitchen with Joan Kekst

PASSOVER COOKERY
In the Kitchen with Joan Kekst

by
Joan Kekst

PHOTOGRAPHY BY
Peter Renerts

© Copyright 2001

PUBLISHED BY
Five Star Publications, Inc.
Chandler, Arizona

Five Star Publications, Inc.
P.O. Box 6698
Chandler, AZ 85246-6698
(480) 940-8182 Fax (480) 940-8787
e-mail: info@FiveStarSupport.com
www.FiveStarSupport.com/passovercookery

First Edition
Library of Congress Cataloging-in-Publication Data

Kekst, Joan, 1933-
    Passover Cookery: in the Kitchen with Joan Kekst p. cm.
    ISBN   1-877749-44-3
        1. Passover cookery. 2. Low-fat diet—Recipes. I. Title

TX739.2.P37 K45 2001
641.5'676—dc21   00-052840
Printed in Canada

10 9 8 7 6 5 4 3 2 1

Published by
Five Star Publications, Inc.
P.O. Box 6698
Chandler, AZ 85246-6698
(480) 940-8182 Fax (480) 940-8787
website: www.FiveStarSupport.com/passovercookery

Electronic version
www.eBookery.com

Crustless Apple Pie
This recipe is adapted with the permission of Scribner, a Division of Simon & Schuster from *The Pie and Pastry Bible* by Rose Levy Beranbaum, Text Copyright © 1998 by Cordon Rose, Inc.

Cordon Rose Cheesecake
This recipe is adapted with the permission of the author from *The Cake Bible* by Rose Levy Beranbaum, Text Copyright ©1988 by Cordon Rose, Inc., published by William Morrow & Co.

CREDITS

PUBLISHER
Linda F. Radke

BOOK DESIGN
Barbara Kordesh

PHOTOGRAPHER
Peter Renerts

PROOFREADERS
Arnold Friedman
Sue DeFabis

INDEXER
Joy Dean Lee

ACKNOWLEDGEMENTS

MY THANKS TO Rabbis Alan Lettofsky, Rabbi Moshe Adler and Rabbi Armond E. Cohen for their knowledge, advice and encouragement during this project. Thank you to Cindy Dettelbach, Editor of the Cleveland Jewish News, and to the paper's many faithful readers who often requested a recipe collection and guide to Passover. Thank you Sybil Kaplan for your kind words.

I am indebted to the dietitians who created the nutritional analysis of recipes for my classes at University Hospitals' Culinary Institute. I am very appreciative of Linda Radke of Five Star Publications, Barbara Kordesh, graphic designer, and Linda's outstanding staff who helped prepare Passover Cookery in record time.

A big thank you to my students, family and friends, who asked the critical questions, contributed their recipes and time to test, taste and prepare foods for my talented photographer, Peter Renerts. Thank you Imogene for your tireless, capable kitchen hands. Many fine recipes get whisked into one's kitchen repertoire; neglected credits are unintentional.

To my children, my sister and my husband who indulged me in *Passover Cookery*, my love and gratitude for your talents, suggestions, critiques and particularly for eating 'Kosher L' Pesach' all these months.

Our remarkable parents and grandparents kept and shared the beauty of Judaism. You make our lives and our Seder table this night, different from all others.

"In every generation . . .

Illustration by Amy Kekst

DEDICATION

To Keeva, My Everything

CONTENTS

FOREWORD

OVER TWENTY YEARS AGO, I went to my mother-in-law's house to help her pack away the Passover dishes after the annual holiday. As we closed the last box, she turned to me and said, "Okay, put them in your car. It's your turn, from now on."

I proudly toted home the ancient dishes, pots, pans and miscellaneous Passover stuff. My husband and I sadly noted the end of an era as I stored the boxes with my grandmother's smaller, even more antique collection.

The weeks before 'my first' Seder were nerve wracking. I cowered at the thought of that first Seder—horrified of making mistakes. The beginning was anything but easy.

Ultimately, initiating our own Seders in conjunction with adult study taught me Passover is much more. It's like a spiritual metamorphosis of house, kitchen culture, food as symbols, personal ritual, and Jewish history. Over time, our family Seders have become legendary.

Looking back, I empathize with today's busy, young homemakers, who live away from family or who are new to Judaism, as well as the next generation that will someday take over making their family Seder for the first time.

The kitchen is a friendly place to talk. During my cooking classes, students openly discussed the fearsome thought of making their own Seder. Passover itself seemed an awesome task. Students of all ages, especially those with young, growing families, were in need of answers to their own Passover questions as well as good guidelines to follow while making their own Seder. Everyone wanted to re-create the warmth of nostalgic childhood memories, yet few had any recollection. They coined the phrase 'tradition-deficient' and declared that they had to start entirely on their own.

And yes, Passover and a Seder must be *made*. It may seem easier today because of many prepared 'Kosher for Passover' items, cookbooks, workshops and an Internet overflowing with advice and recipes. Despite the fact that a Passover Seder is the most highly observed Jewish home ritual, making your own Seder for the first time *is* a daunting task.

The biggest mistake would be *not* to make a Seder. Seder means order, and if you approach Passover understanding its orderly configuration and unique goals, your fears should disappear. Rabbis structured the Seder experience as a family lesson at the table, with devices to effectively engage family members and to make each one personally feel part of the ancient, Exodus event. Passover is different, not difficult. Only the beginning is hard.

Over the years, most Seders spawn their own traditions. Certain symbolic foods cue the Passover story while ethnic foods relate a family's history. For me cooking beyond our Eastern European origins and baking without *leaven* is an ever-present challenge. As I experiment with other ethnic or new recipes, our children critique, chiding me to keep the same menu. Indeed some dishes are now standard on our Seder menu.

We love the weeks before the Seder, as our five children, their spouses and our grandchildren shift furniture, unpack and wash Grandma's aging chipped dishes, glassware and huge pots. I recall how my grandmother even cooked in a certain order. First she used her one big "good" pot to make gefilte fish so later it could be used for the soup. She had to—she only had one large pot. And here I am, following a similar routine with her pot. Our invited guests often drop by and fall into the routine of peeling potatoes and carrots or separating eggs. Our grandchildren exclaim when our eldest son grates the horseradish and gives them a whiff. They chop *Charoset* and make place cards to assure they will get their favorite dish from my grandmother's aged collection, like my cousins and I and their mothers used to do. The table abounds with their handmade school art and jumping frogs when Ten Plagues are recited. Oh yes, there are always a few unexpected guests to squeeze in.

We don't lay claim to any extraordinary creative methods of storytelling, but everyone at our huge table joins in to read every word and sing every song from the Haggadah. The annual gathering of family and close friends, coupled with the performance of the same rituals, established our family traditions. Everyone anticipates the holiday as an annual highlight. Perhaps the annual preparations, which mirror our family history, rival being together at the Passover Seder table.

Whether your family has long-standing traditions or is observing the holiday for the first time, find comfortable methods that make the narrative come alive for everyone. Different devices work for different families. In one friend's family, each year one of their married children conducts and directs the Seder, with different innovations. Another family gets up and treks around the house to recall the Israelites' sojourn in the desert. Our grandchildren contribute artistic place cards and their hand made matzo covers and seder plates. Recruit help and suggestions for Seder activities from family and guests, especially the children.

No matter how foreboding the thought of making my first Seder was, Passover became and remains the climax of our family's Jewish holiday celebrations. I have enormous gratitude for my mother-in-law who graciously handed over "making Passover" while she could still be at our table. If I made a mistake, she never said a word.

Starting your own customs may seem a lofty challenge. Don't be afraid of mistakes— they are all merely learning experiences. The unusual Passover foods at the Seder often seem to be the challenge. In fact, the core requirements of the Seder are quite simple. The stars of the festive meal are the children and those seated at your table. Annually, each Seder creates its own special quality to become a wonderful future Passover memory for your children and grandchildren.

PASSOVER COMMEMORATES the Israelite Exodus from Egyptian bondage to liberty in the Promised Land. The Torah instructs Jews to remember their history…how because of a great famine, the Jews went down to Egypt…how they were enslaved to build Pharaoh's stone houses…how Moses heard God's voice and asked Pharaoh to let his people go…how Pharaoh increased their hardships, until Ten Plagues came upon Egypt…how the Angel of Death did "pass over" the Hebrews' houses…how the Red Sea parted so the Israelites walked on dry land, carrying troughs of unleavened bread…how the Israelites wandered forty years until coming to the Promised Land.

At Passover, our sages urge Jews to intellectually and emotionally encounter slavery. Annually, for over 3,000 years, at evening on the 14th day in the Hebrew month of Nisan, Jewish families recount the Exodus event to become more than a remote experience of slavery for the sake of memory alone. The concept of personal freedom and the sovereignty of our People are a vigil for all generations to keep.

Passover incorporates even earlier traditions. Once, an annual agricultural festival coincided with the first spring barley harvest. People were instructed to discard the old flour and over-ripe perpetual pot of chometz, leavening (yeast). Annually casting out leaven gives Matzo multiple meanings—from the bread of purity to the bread of affliction and ultimately the bread of freedom.

At another ancient ceremony, Jewish shepherds sacrificed the first-born lamb at a spring Festival of the Paschal Lamb. In ancient Israel, Jews observed Passover as one of three Pilgrimages to Jerusalem when the Kohanim offered sacrifices at the Great Temple to celebrate the spring festival of the new lamb and the new season. Since the Roman destruction of Jerusalem's Great Temple in 70 CE, the Paschal lamb is no longer sacrificed.

Only the Passover Pilgrimage to Jerusalem also required women to undertake the journey. The Torah decreed, over time the Talmud interpreted and rabbis structured our Passover observances to focus in each Jewish home. At Passover many Jewish women still undertake a type of Passover pilgrimage as they create their families' home celebration. Thus, in Jewish homes around the world, each table becomes an altar.

The order of home preparations is Biblically commanded as well as the order at the Seder table and the meal itself. New rituals reflect how the Jewish people recapture their Biblical heritage and continue to glean new meanings as they perform rituals from our forefathers and foremothers. Before looking at a single recipe or counting the chairs and invited guests, one should understand and know how to distinguish the Seder meal and days of Passover from all other days.

> "...Seven days thou shalt eat unleavened bread...no leavened bread shall be seen with thee..."
>
> —EXODUS 13:7

Chometz, (leaven), has a twofold commandment. Chometz should be neither seen nor "found" in our homes on Passover. Today, if leavened products remain in Jewish homes at the holiday, a modern solution is adopted. Originally used for German Jewish beer makers, known as a "legal fiction", leavened products are removed not only from the kitchen, but the entire house and locked in a remote place during Passover. Sold by a Rabbinic authority to a non-Jew for the duration of the holiday, the sale is dissolved after Passover.

A Chometz Search is made the night before, except on Shabbat, then it is two nights before or if necessary, by 10 a.m. the morning of the first Seder. After an appropriate prayer, crumbs are ceremoniously burned to declare that chometz does not exist in this house and its family is ready to celebrate Passover. (Children love to help grandparents and parents at this old-fashioned ceremony— do save some crumbs for it.)

The Seder is the highlight of Passover. The essential elements are commanded at an "ordered" feast—to eat of the roasted Paschal lamb together with unleavened bread, bitter herbs and to tell the story of the Exodus in response to our children's queries. Later, Talmudic sages added two more requirements: Four Celebratory Cups of Wine and the Hallel, a recitation of Biblical Psalms praising God's redemptive miracles. Together these five actions construct the core of a Seder making it a true educational event and inspirational experience.

Four Questions beg the story of the Exodus to be told. Traditionally, the youngest child present asks the questions. Answers flow from the Haggadah in a manner so all from the simplest to the wisest, the youngest to the eldest, will understand the events of the Exodus.

The Haggadah, Hebrew for telling, is an instructional manual written in both Hebrew and the common local language, so each Seder participant can read a portion from the Haggadah. The Haggadah prompts the Seder's procedures and tells the Exodus story. As the narrative unfolds, participants are cued to consume symbolic foods to emphasize the events of the Exodus.

Recently published, creative and artistically designed *Haggadot* (plural for Haggadah) feature themes and ideas for children, families or feminists, often posing questions for family discussions. Selecting the "right" Haggadah is important. It's appropriate that everyone use the same edition so all can follow and participate.

THE SEDER PLATE is the ceremonial centerfold and the essence of a Passover Seder. It contains six items, two of which are not required to be tasted. Each table has its own Seder Plate and symbolic foods to sample. Small Seder plates for each child are especially nice.

SYMBOLIC SEDER PLATE FOODS CUE THE STORY

Karpas, parsley or a green vegetable, symbolizes the rebirth of Spring.

Moror, a bitter herb, is the bitter base of romaine lettuce or fresh horseradish root.

Charoset, Hebrew for clay, is a mixture of fruits, spices, nuts and Passover wine to connote the mortar used by Hebrew slaves in Egypt. Various ingredients compose ethnic family recipes, a simultaneous reminder of slavery and the sweetness of freedom.

Mayim Melech, salt water, is used to dip and recall tears shed as Israelite slaves.

Zeroa, a roasted lamb shank, symbolic of the ancient sacrifice, is not eaten.

Betzah, a roasted egg, also not eaten, recalls Temple sacrifices and symbolizes life.

Three slices of matzo are set on the table. At the appropriate time, the middle matzo is broken and hidden. Known as the Afikomen, Greek for dessert, this matzo is required to complete the Seder. The boisterous hunt for it keeps the children involved, until the Sedermaster rewards them. The Afikomen is the last food eaten to prolong the Seder's flavor.

The Core of the Seder

Transliterated from Hebrew in the Haggadah, the Seder evolved approximately as follows:

Kadesh • Kiddush, prayer over wine to declare the festival's holiness.

Ur-chatz • Ritual hand-washing.

Karpas • Eat a green vegetable, dipped in salt water.

Yachatz • Break the middle matzo, hide a piece (the Afikomen) to be redeemed at the meal's conclusion.

Magid • Recitation of the Exodus story and begin recitation of the Hallel.

Rachatzah • Main hand-washing ritual to eat unleavened bread and the festive meal.

Motzi • The usual blessing to thank God for bread is used over matzo.

Maror • Blessing over the bitter herb and eating it.

Korech • Eating a sandwich of bitter herbs, in memory of original Paschal lamb.

Shulchan Orech • Serve the festive meal.

Tzafun • Find the "hidden" matzo. The Afikomen, dessert, is the last Seder food.

Barech • Grace after meals.

Hallel • Complete a recitation of the Psalms.

Nirtzah • Concluding prayer, asks God to accept the service we lovingly offer.

UNIQUE PASSOVER CUSTOMS

In most Jewish homes, some or all of the following customs will be observed.

Two Sedarim are performed by most Jews, except in Israel.

The Sedermaster or Sedermistress is the person who leads the assemblage in the ritual ceremonies.

Candles are lit 18 minutes before sundown. At our Seder women of each family light candles together.

Standing or Reclining to the left on a pillow, the Sedermaster and other celebrants symbolically dine as free men did in the ancient middle east.

Kiddush is the blessing said over the first cup of wine.

Miriam's Cup of water, placed on some tables, recalls how the prophetess led the women to rejoice after crossing the Sea.

Schmira Matzo is literally guarded from harvest through baking and reserved on a tray for the Three Matzo.

Elijah's Cup brims with wine. A child opens the door to usher in his presence near the Seder's end. Peek at the cup—there is less wine! All stand to sing *Eliahu Anevi*, in praise.

Kepah is a head covering, usually provided for each male.

Hand Washing is performed by the Sedermaster with a cup and bowl to ritually wash hands before eating, as the Kohanim (priests) once did.

Eggs and Salt Water is a first course, reminiscent of mixed blessings, life and its tears.

Fresh Flowers are a lovely custom, the harbingers of spring.

White Tablecloth is reminiscent of the desert sands Jews wandered for forty years.

Guests are invited. Let all who are hungry come and eat. No one should be alone at Passover.

"KOSHER FOR PASSOVER"

The week of Passover tests the kosher cook to the utmost. Added to the already complex Jewish dietary laws, Biblical law prohibits many normally kosher foods during Passover. These include any food containing chometz from wheat, rye, oats, spelt, barley or corn and their derivative products. Fermented foods made from a grain alcohol are also prohibited.

Various ethnic groups follow different food traditions. Ashkenazim, Jews of German or East European descent, do not partake of several foods that Sephardim, Jews of Spanish or Oriental descent, eat during the holiday. Adopted by a group of pietistic Ashkenaziim in the twelfth and thirteenth centuries, they chose to deprive themselves of foods that were actually permitted. Refraining from legumes, corn and rice, which look like grains, is an enduring custom. Oriental Jews claim rice does not ferment so they use rice and other grains. Thus, while some recipes are accepted by certain ethnic groups, others will not be. It's important to define and to establish your own ethnic traditions as your family begins Passover observances.

Packaged Food Purchases

Generally, packaged Passover foods are marked with a rabbinic seal of supervision and date for use during the current Passover holiday. Some normally kosher packaged foods do not need special labels if purchased before the holiday and kept unopened until Passover preparations begin. If purchased during Passover, the same items need a label.

If purchased before Passover, foods that do not need a label include: pure coffee, tea, non-iodized salt, pepper, spices, honey, sugar, butter, eggs, nuts, olive oil, pure frozen fruits and vegetables (except legumes), fresh fruits, vegetables including green beans and fresh herbs.

Products that always require a Passover label include: vanilla and other flavorings, (by-products of grain alcohol), baking soda, confectioners' sugar (made with potato starch), canned goods, margarine (use *pareve* in meat recipes), yogurt, cream, cheeses, wines, liqueurs, dried fruits, coconut, chocolate, oils, vinegar, soda, juices, and candy. Some ethnic groups prohibit certain herbs in pods and mustard seeds.

Obviously, various levels of observance exist. Consult your rabbi, Jewish Community Center or a list of published Passover products from a known kosher source.

The Passover Ingredients

Most American Jewish cooks use matzo, the humble bread of affliction, in various forms. Some Jews do not allow any matzo product to contact a liquid as it always swells. Generally, recipes requiring matzo products, including matzo farfel, matzo meal, matzo cake meal and potato starch, are basic to Passover cuisine. Matzo cake meal combined with potato starch is a common flour substitute (and thickener) in Passover baking and cooking.

These products work a little differently. If using them for the first time, remember they continue to absorb liquid, need generous flavoring and should be worked quickly in baking. Annually, experienced bakers have at least one cake failure. Be patient and practice with these unique ingredients.

Carefully calculate amounts of matzo products to purchase as some sell-out quickly. Conversely, don't over-buy. Matzo meal and matzo cake meal, easily used all year, are expensive. Better, less costly products are available after the holiday.

Kosher gelatin is available. Not as firm as ordinary gelatin. Stir into cold liquid to dissolve, then slowly heat. It sets quickly, so add remaining ingredients immediately.

Eggs are a major leavening agent in Passover baking, the base that holds numerous ingredients together.

Potato starch thickens best dissolved in cold water. Heat slowly or add to warm liquids.

ABOUT THE RECIPES

All recipes are kosher—if kosher for Passover meats, fish and purchased products are used. Recipes are labeled meat, dairy or pareve. As with any cuisine, it's important to use the freshest possible fruit, vegetables, herbs, top-quality meats, fish and other fine products. Recipes span traditional and contemporary Passover foods, low fat, vegetarian preferences, and children's favorites.

The extra chores and invited guests place time constraints on busy homemakers at Passover. Practical menus should include recipes that can be doubled or partially prepared in advance and some to serve at room temperature. Recipes to double and to make ahead in stages to refrigerate or freeze are included and noted. Many cakes freeze well, if properly wrapped. They are best frosted after defrosting.

EAT HEARTILY—IN GOOD HEALTH

Food is obviously important in our family—so is health. Like so many other people, personal health conditions made us aware how serious proper eating is to one's well being. An occasional meal of excess may not be harmful but a whole week of Passover foods can send cholesterol and fat levels seriously out of control. Numerous low-fat fish courses, vegetables and soups are included for healthier options.

Where possible, recipes indicate how to eliminate up to 20 percent of the egg yolks with little change in quality. Replace the volume with additional egg whites plus 1 teaspoon water. If a recipe requires all the protein, substitute each eliminated yolk with one egg white plus 1 tablespoon thick applesauce or 1 teaspoon vegetable oil. Ingredients remain cohesive and the texture only suffers slightly. Test recipes and make your own notations. I included my results.

Replace whole milk with skim milk; replace cheeses with low-fat cheese if available or homemade "yogurt cheese". Avoid egg matzo. Garnish meats with fruit or vegetables.

Reduce nuts by 1/3 the suggested amount if nuts are used for flavor and texture. If nuts are a major dry ingredient (a piecrust or cake), reduce only 10 percent.

Substitute 3 T cocoa powder plus 1 tablespoon low-fat margarine for 1 ounce of solid unsweetened chocolate to lower cholesterol content. Fruit and sorbet are the best options. *The above information was developed in cooperation with The American Heart Association.*

I reduce a portion of the egg yolks in gefilte fish and matzo balls. The results are good, but not always perfect. Additional whites successfully substitute 20 percent of the yolks in traditional gefilte fish. Matzo balls are more dependent on egg yolks and fat for their cohesiveness. Substitute only 10 percent of the yolks with egg whites plus ½ teaspoon oil per yolk.

Well-made soup stock is a critical base for low fat soups, sauces and gravy. Vegetable and chicken stocks, always great cooking assets, are especially important in the Passover kitchen. Make vegetable stock, generously flavor and freeze. Defrost, simply add choices of fresh vegetables and herbs.

Likewise defatted chicken stock accepts many flavors, and of course, floats the marvelous matzo ball. Reduced chicken stock is the essence of sauces to coat poultry with an enticing gloss and convey endless flavors from fresh herbs and wine, to citrus or vegetables.

Reduce and strain stocks then add salt to minimize sodium content. Freeze defatted chicken or vegetable stock in pint zip-lock plastic bags. It defrosts quickly for a multitude of uses.

I developed these cooking methods to accommodate my husband's cardiovascular conditions. Teaching classes at The Culinary Institute, their dietitians created the nutrient analysis for my recipes in classes. Careful, healthful cooking has become a way of life for us and many other families.

Passover Baking

Passover desserts seem especially laden with eggs. Where possible, a reduction in egg yolks in favor of egg whites is indicated. Healthful substitutions are used in many Passover dessert recipes and still produce satisfactory flavors. Select fresh or cooked fruit confections and sorbet for the lowest fat dessert options.

Annually, newly certified kosher for Passover products appear on the market. (Consult websites for suppliers and order early.) Recently improved egg substitute, non-dairy creamer and whipped topping are available and quite useful in general cooking rather than baking. Powdered egg whites are an excellent Passover product. Available in the kosher section of supermarkets or at kosher butcher shops, they are easy to use and beat well for baking, an enormous help to the cholesterol conscious cook.

Recipes call for large eggs unless otherwise specified. Passover vanilla or confectioner's sugar may be in short supply. Packets of vanilla sugar are available or bury a vanilla bean in 2 cups of sugar to steep and flavor cakes. (Remove the volume of vanilla sugar used from measured amount). Recipes offer suggestions and detailed directions to assist the novice baker in properly beating egg whites, as eggs are a major leavening agent in most cakes.

COUNTDOWN TO PASSOVER

The Seder is a family experience—Passover preparations should be also. Invite the whole family to participate. For first-timers the following outline can be helpful.

Six Weeks Ahead

- Make a master list and reserve time for major household chores; share with family members.

- Repair or replace required electrical cords, appliances or other household items.

- Inventory chairs, tables, plates, glasses, utensils, pots, pans, linen, flatware. Buy new processor bowl, beaters and plastic storage containers as needed. (square ones are refrigerator-efficient.)

- Defrost and clean freezer early.

- Check Haggadot and Kepot; Check Seder plates, candles, wineglasses. Purchase, borrow or consider disposable items.

- Arrange to hire helpers if possible; order necessary rental items.

Four Weeks Ahead

- Plan daily menus to use up *chometz* from pantry and freezer.

- Review the ritual manner to render certain *chometz* items "Kosher L' Pesach".

- Invite guests; remind family of work schedule.

- Attend Passover workshop or cooking class if desired.

- Empty, clean and reserve some kitchen cabinets for Passover items.

- Plan Seder menus, select recipes and foods to cook ahead.

- Make an early list to shop for staples, paper goods, and candles to ease the budget crunch. Order kosher wine.

- Arrange family practice of the Haggadah. Urge children to prepare artwork, questions or develop their simulations of the Passover story.

Two to Three Weeks Ahead

- Check recipes for specialty items; visit kosher markets for new Passover items.

- As time permits, *kasher* (ritually clean) pots and pans for advance cooking and store in clean cupboard. *Kasher* oven, stovetop and counter for early Passover cooking if possible.

- Purchase ingredients to advance cook foods that freeze well: chicken soup, sorbet, kugels, brisket, sauced chicken breasts and some cakes.

- Tell guests who wish to help when to come to cook, or what kosher items to bring.

- Check, clean or launder clothing and linens for Seder as necessary.

One Week Ahead

- Schedule and complete major cooking to freeze. Make extra ice.
- Purchase vegetable staples, potatoes, onions, carrots, dried fruits, nuts, soda pop.
- Line storage cabinets and counters; clean refrigerator, reserve area for Chometz.
- Wash Passover pots/pans, dishes glassware, flatware, candlesticks, Seder plate.

Five Days Ahead

- Consult your rabbi to sell your Chometz.
- Purchase least perishable fruits, vegetables, dairy, eggs, Seder plate items.
- Make horseradish, bake cookies, freeze or store air-tight; make fruit compote.
- Shift furniture to accommodate extra tables and chairs.
- Prepare rooms for-out-of-town guests.

One to Three Days Ahead

- Use up all open chometz; except crumbs for ceremonial "search".
- Let children place extra chairs, spread cloths on tables, set out dishes.
- Complete baking, partially prepare long-cooking items, chill to re-heat, store airtight or freeze.

- Make gefilte or other fish; mix batter for matzo balls, chill overnight.
- Purchase last-minute perishable vegetables and fruits.
- Fill and cork wine decanters; defrost frozen items in refrigerator.

On the Seder Day

- Search for and burn chometz; none should be eaten after 10 a.m. the Seder day.
- Roast bone and egg for Seder Plate, hard boil eggs for salt water, make Charoset.
- Prepare fresh vegetables and fruits, frost cakes, boil matzo balls.
- Set food on platters, cover and refrigerate. Plan oven timing to heat food.
- Save one hour to bathe and rest!
- Keep an inventory for next year!

Have a Sweet Happy Holiday!
CHAG SAMEACH!

THE SEDER TABLE

"SEVEN DAYS THOU SHALT EAT UNLEAVENED BREAD...THE FIRST DAY YOU SHALL PUT AWAY LEAVEN, OUT OF YOUR HOUSES..."

—EXODUS 12:15

EVERY SEDER REQUIRES:

- Kiddush Wine
- Seder Plate Items
- Matzo
- Eggs and Salt Water
- Elijah's Cup
- Water Pitcher, Bowl and Towel

PASSOVER SEDER MENUS

SEDER I

Gefilte Fish with Horseradish
Chicken Soup with Mini Matzo Balls
Festive Fruited Beef Brisket
  or Roasted Stuffed Capon
Potato Knishes with Caramelized Onions
Pale Green Spring Salad
Roasted Cauliflower with Red Onions
Chocolate Elegance Cake with Mousse
Stewed Fruit Compote

SEDER II

Sephardic Fish in Tomato Sauce
Beet Borscht with Flanken and Matzo Farfel
Chicken Roulade with Scallion Sauce
  or Turkey Schnitzel
Potato Zucchini Kugel
Brussels Sprouts with Chestnuts
Roasted Beets and Onion Salad
Passover Turkish Nut Torte
Honey Roasted Pears

VEGETARIAN SEDER

Baked Garlic Carp
Golden Noodle Vegetable Soup
Stuffed Sweet Red Peppers
  or Eggplant Moussaka
Potato and Carrot Tsimmes
Garlicky Tomato Salad
Roasted Asparagus with Sweet Pepper Confetti
Rich Chocolate Torte
Orange Slices with Moroccan Spices

LOW CHOLESTEROL SEDER

Steamed Halibut in Romaine Leaves
Chicken Broth with Vegetables Julienne
Game Hens with Plum Sauce
  or Golden Turkey Breast
Honey Glazed Carrots
Sweet Onion Slaw
Low Fat Potato Kugel
Low Fat Pineapple Sponge Cake
Poached Pears in Red Raspberry Sauce

SEDER TABLE
CEREMONIAL FOODS

CHAROSET RECIPES COMPILED FROM VARIOUS SOURCES.

SEVEN DAY PASSOVER EGGS

12	or more eggs
1/4	lb. red onion skins
6 to 8	medium bay leaves
1	T dry basil
1	T black peppercorns
3	T olive oil
2	T kosher salt

This old-world Sephardic recipe symbolizes fertility and rebirth. Deeply colored, hard cooked eggs suggest the dark, difficult life of slavery. The egg, a strong motif during Passover, promises new life. They are shared at the table or given away.

Place half the red onion skins in a heavy pot large enough to hold eggs. Add eggs, black pepper, bay leaves, basil and olive oil. Cover generously with cold water, let steep one hour.

Add remaining red onion skins. Slowly bring to a boil over low heat. Reduce to lowest setting, cover, only allow to simmer. Add warm water as needed. Eggs may be simmered up 7 days, however 36 hours is adequate. Chill until ready to use.

ASHKENAZI CHAROSET

MAKES ABOUT **3** CUPS	
6	apples, peeled, cored
1	cup walnuts or almonds
1	tsp. ground cinnamon
	Grated rind of one lemon
1/2	cup red wine

Chop fruits and nuts, mix well. Add cinnamon, lemon juice and wine. Store in a glass jar. (We double this to use as a spread on matzo crackers.)

WINE CUPS ARE FILLED FOUR TIMES DURING THE SEDER

My grandmother gave me this nineteenth century wine cup which she brought from Russia.

EGYPTIAN CHAROSET

MAKES 2 CUPS

- 8 oz. pitted dates, chopped
- 8 oz. golden raisins
- 1/2 cup sweet red Passover wine
- 1/2 cup almonds, coarsely chopped

Simmer dates and raisins in a small saucepan with the wine and enough water to cover, on low heat. Stir occasionally until dates become mushy and thicken into a paste. Spoon into a bowl and sprinkle with almonds.

ISRAELI CHAROSET

MAKES 7 CUPS

- 1 lb. fresh pitted dates
- 1 lb. golden raisins
- 3/4 lb. almonds
- 1/2 lb. walnuts
- 3 whole pomegranates, peeled, remove seeds
- 1 T spices, cinnamon, pepper, cumin, cardamom, cloves, ginger
- 3/4 cup red wine

Chop fruits and nuts, add spices and red wine. Adjust flavor to taste.

MORROCCAN CHAROSET

YIELDS 5 CUPS

- 25 dates, pitted and chopped
- 1/2 cup pistachio nuts, unsalted
- 1/2 cup almonds
- 1/2 cup golden raisins
- 2 apples, peeled, cored and diced
- 1 pomegranate, juiced
- 1 orange, peeled and chopped
- 1 banana, sliced
- 3/4 cup sweet red wine
- 3 T cider vinegar
- 1 T black pepper, 1/2 T cayenne pepper, or to taste
- 1 T each, ground cloves, cardamom and cinnamon

Combine fruits and nuts, finely chop or grind in a food processor. Add wine, pomegranate juice and vinegar to make a paste. Blend in spices. Store in a glass jar in refrigerator.

ITALIAN CHAROSET

Finely chop dates, walnuts, apples and orange into a bowl. Mash banana, add with wine, lemon juice and spices, mix well. Add matzo meal as needed. Italians make the charoset into tiny balls to pass at the table.

MAKES 2 CUPS

1/2	lb. pitted dates
1/2	lb. walnuts
3	large apples
1	large seedless orange
1	large banana
1/2	cup sweet Malaga wine
1/2	tsp. cinnamon
1/8	tsp. ground cloves
1	T lemon juice
	matzo meal as needed

TURKISH CHAROSET

Simmer all ingredients except walnuts and sugar in a medium saucepan on low heat until very soft. Add sugar to taste. Cool slightly and blend in processor. Add walnuts.

MAKES 3 CUPS

1/2	lb. (2) sweet red apples
1/2	lb. pitted dates
1	cup raisins
1	orange, juice and grated zest
3	T sugar, or more
1	cup Passover wine
1/4	cup walnuts, chopped

CHAROSET RECIPES COMPILED FROM VARIOUS ETHNIC SOURCES.

Roasting the Zeroa • Place the shank bone of a lamb on a piece of foil in a 400° F oven. Roast, turning occasionally, for about one hour, until very browned.

Betzah • During the last 30 minutes of roasting the shank bone, puncture a raw or hard boiled egg and roast it on the foil with the bone until very brown.

Moror • Reserve the horseradish top with a piece of its white root for the Seder plate. The base of Romaine lettuce is also bitter or use strong onions. Cut extras and place around the Seder table.

Eggs and Salt Water • Use one egg for every two persons, plus a few extra. Hard cook eggs several hours ahead, run under cool water, peel while warm. Chop and cover with cold water, heavily salted, just before serving. Serve small portions to each person. I toss out about half the yolks.

Halibut Wrapped in Romaine

Drummettes and Wings—Polkes and Fligels

FIRST COURSES

"WE REMEMBER THE FISH, WHICH WE ATE IN EGYPT FOR NOTHING;

THE CUCUMBERS, AND THE MELONS, AND THE LEEKS, AND THE ONIONS,

AND THE GARLIC..." —**NUMBERS 11:5**

TRADITIONAL GEFILTE FISH - Pareve

YIELDS: 24 TO 30 FISH BALLS

8 lb. fresh ground fish; combination of white fish, yellow pike, perch; reserve bones and heads

5 onions; 2 sliced and 3 grated

6 carrots, peeled

8 eggs **or** 4 whole eggs and 5 egg whites, beaten with 4 T water

1/2 tsp. sugar

2 tsp. kosher salt, 8 white peppercorns, to taste

1 to 1¼ cup matzo meal

1 to 1¼ cup water

parsley or dill sprigs to garnish platter

The long debate on cooking gefilte fish balls continues; two ways are included. I prefer the second method. To make gefilte fish ahead, carefully follow storage directions to avoid spoilage.

Drain excess liquid from the 3 grated onions. Place in a large mixing bowl. Combine with ground fish, 1 grated carrot, beaten eggs, sugar, 1 tsp. salt, ground white pepper and 1 cup matzo meal. Mix well, stir in 1 cup water. Let stand 10 minutes. Mixture may be loose due to reduced egg yolks; add more matzo meal by the spoonful, mix thoroughly. If mixture is stiff, add remaining water in small amounts. Allow mixture to stand; prepare the pot.

Option One: Thoroughly rinse bones and heads in cold water. Place bones in a heavy 10 quart stockpot with 1 sliced onion, 1 chunked carrot, several parsley sprigs, ½ tsp. salt and several peppercorns. Add 4 qt. cold water, bring to a simmer for 20 minutes. Remove from heat, cool. Strain broth into clean pot, discard bones and vegetables. Add remaining carrots and onion, ½ tsp. salt, peppercorns and set over low heat.

Option Two: Place rinsed bones and heads on bottom of pot. Add 2 sliced onions, 4 whole carrots, 1 tsp. salt, pepper and 3 qt. cold water.

Moisten hands to form fish balls with about ⅓ cup of fish mixture. For either method, gently cushion fish balls on vegetables or the bones in pot, over medium heat. Add fish balls in layers, rotate pot to moisten balls. Taste fish juices, adjust salt and pepper. Cover and cook at a simmer about 2 hours. Occasionally rotate pot to moisten fish.

When cool enough to handle, remove fish balls with a wooden spoon, to platter. Cut carrot slices to garnish each ball; cover with plastic and chill.

Strain fish broth for chowder or gelatin. For gelatin, simmer fish juices, to reduce by half. Chill in a shallow glass pan. Cut in cubes to garnish fish.

Note: MY FRIEND RENEE GOODMAN GAVE ME THIS HUGE HELP TO MAKE FISH ONE WEEK AHEAD. IMMEDIATELY PLACE HOT FISH IN HOT, STERILE GLASS JARS. STRAIN BOILING HOT BROTH OVER FISH, TILT JAR TO RELEASE AIR BUBBLES. CRUMPLE A PIECE OF WAX PAPER TO KEEP FISH SUBMERGED. CAP WITH A RUBBER, AIRTIGHT LID. COOL. CHILL UP TO 10 DAYS.

GEFILTE FISH VARIATIONS

SALMON STEAKS STUFFED with GEFILTE FISH - Pareve

SERVES 8

- 8 small salmon steaks, 1" thick
- 1 large carrot, sliced
- 1 medium onion, chopped
- 1 inch strip of lemon zest
- 1 tsp. salt; several peppercorns pinch of sugar
- 1 lb. ground fish
- 2 egg whites
- 1/2 cup matzo meal
- 1/4 cup cold water
- 4 sprigs fresh dill, more for garnish

I met Madame Lila Mandelman in the Marais area of Paris, at the Deli. I commented on the gefilte fish she was eating. Our conversation resulted in an invitation to her home, a correspondence and her gefilte fish recipe.

In a wide, deep pot, preferably with a rack, place 3 qt. water, carrot, onion, lemon zest, salt, peppercorns and a pinch of sugar. Simmer 15 minutes.

Meanwhile, combine the ground fish, egg whites and matzo meal. Add 2 T cold water. If mixture is very thick, add more water. Season with salt and pepper.

Rinse salmon steaks, pat dry. Remove the large center bone. Lightly season with salt and pepper. Divide ground fish mixture into 8 portions. Fill the center of each salmon steak, fasten with a toothpick if needed.

Add the dill to the simmering bouillon. Lower salmon steaks into bouillon, in a single layer. Return to a simmer, cover and remove from heat. Allow fish to steep 20 minutes. Gently remove with a slotted spoon to serving platter. Return bouillon to heat, repeat with remaining fish. Chill overnight. Option, strain and reduce fish broth. Chill for gelatin cubes. Serve at room temperature with white horse-radish and fresh dill.

GEFILTE FISH WRAPPED in CABBAGE LEAVES - Pareve

12 PORTIONS

12 to 14 large cabbage leaves

8 cups prepared fish stock

3 lb. ground fish, reserve bones and trimmings

1 T vegetable oil

1 medium onion, chopped

3 large eggs

3/4 cup matzo meal

3 T finely minced parsley

salt and pepper to taste

1 T cider vinegar

2 large carrots, peeled, cut into julienne

1 large leek, white part only, cut into julienne

1/2 cup freshly peeled, grated, horseradish slivers

Steam cabbage leaves over lightly salted water about 5 minutes, pat dry. Trim thick ends at stem, set aside. Strain prepared fish stock, keep at a simmer.

Cook onion in oil until translucent. Combine in a bowl with ground fish, eggs, matzo meal, parsley, about 1 cup fish stock and season with salt and pepper.

Divide fish mixture onto cabbage leaves. Roll to completely enclose fish mixture. Bring remaining fish stock to a boil in a large heavy stockpot. Add 1 T cider vinegar and ½ tsp. salt, reduce heat to medium. Lower fish rolls into pot. Sprinkle with carrots and leek. Cover and simmer about 25 to 30 minutes until the cabbage is very tender.

Remove fish with a slotted spoon to serving platter, scatter with vegetables. Serve warm or at room temperature with horseradish slivers.

SPANISH STYLE GEFILTE FISH

MAKES 24 SMALL FISH PATTIES

5 lb. ground fish, white fish and pike

2 medium grated onions

garlic salt, salt and pepper to taste

2 jumbo eggs

1/4 cup matzo meal

2 cans Passover tomato mushroom sauce

oil for frying

My friend Donna Yanowitz made this with her mother Esther Karon. Later her mother-in-law Mollie Yanowitz added tomato sauce and baked the fish patties.

Mix fish, onions, garlic salt, salt and pepper and eggs in a large bowl. Add a bit more matzo meal if needed for a cohesive mixture. Form into patties. Sauté in a small amount of oil until lightly browned on both sides. Arrange patties in a large glass baking pan. May be refrigerated at this point.

Preheat oven to 350° F. Spread tomato mushroom sauce over fish and bake one hour. Fish puffs during baking. Serve hot.

Makes 24 small fish patties. Make larger patties for a main course.

SWEET AND SOUR YELLOW PIKE - Pareve

SERVES 12 PORTIONS

4	lb. yellow pike, cut in 1¹/₂" slices
1¹/₂	cup sugar
¹/₂	cup cider vinegar
2¹/₂	cup water
1	tsp. kosher salt, 6 peppercorns or to taste
3	bay leaves
3	medium sweet white onions, thinly sliced
1	whole lemon, seeded and thinly sliced
1	garlic clove, crushed
¹/₂	cup white raisins, optional

An old European favorite that Aunt Mona Heifetz showed me how to make. My Dad loved it.

❖ ❖ ❖

Slowly heat sugar in a heavy-bottomed 6 qt. stockpot. As it begins to caramelize, rotate pot to prevent scorching. When sugar is a light caramel color, remove from heat, slowly add cider vinegar and water. Return to heat, allow sugar syrup to melt slowly. Add salt, peppercorns, bay leaves, onions, garlic and lemon slices. Simmer 10 minutes.

Rinse fish slices well, add to pot. Cover pot and turn off heat on an electric stove. On a gas stove, allow the liquid to return just to a boil, turn off heat, steep 20 minutes. Carefully lift fish with a slotted spoon to a deep serving platter. Scatter onions and lemon slices over fish.

Strain remaining juices, discard bay leaves and peppercorns, return liquid to clean pot. Simmer, reduce by one-third, add raisins while hot. Cool and pour over fish or chill strained juices in a shallow pan separately to gel.

Can be made three days ahead and refrigerated. Serve fish at room temperature. Watch the bones!

NUTRITIONAL ANALYSIS

Total Calories: 194	Fat: 1g	Carbohydrate: 24g	Sodium: 110mg
Cholesterol: 44mg	Protein: 22g	Alcohol: 0	Alcohol: 0

BECKY'S BAKED CARP - Pareve

SERVES 8 TO 10

6	lb. carp, sliced 1¹/₂" thick
8	garlic cloves, minced
	salt, pepper and garlic powder

Grandma Becky Kekst and my husband devoured her famed carp on Pesach. I make it with our cousin Fred—it's become a contest. No decision, so far.

❖ ❖ ❖

Thoroughly rinse fish, trim fins and large scales. Dry. Season with garlic, salt, pepper and garlic powder. Keep at room temperature up to one hour to absorb flavor.

Preheat oven to 475° F. Line a heavy baking pan with foil. Spray with vegetable spray. Arrange fish slices on tray, not touching. Bake 45 minutes. Reduce temperature to 425° F. Continue baking 35 minutes more until fish is dry and crisp. Remove while warm with a spatula to a glass dish. Cool. Best slightly warm. Refrigerate up to one week. Serve at room temperature.

HALIBUT WRAPPED in ROMAINE - Pareve

MAKES 8 APPETIZER PORTIONS

8 pieces (4oz.) halibut fillets
   or similar fish

1 lemon

3 T olive oil

1/2 cups leeks, white only,
     minced

1/2 cup red onion, minced

3 garlic cloves, sliced

   salt and pepper to taste

3/4 cup fish stock **or** water

1 T red wine vinegar

16 fresh romaine leaves,
    trim core

    lemon slices, mint leaves
    to garnish

Rinse fillets, pat dry. Squeeze the juice of half a lemon over fillets, season well with salt and pepper. In a medium sauté pan, heat 2 T oil, sauté leeks 5 minutes until translucent. Add onions, sauté 2 minutes, add garlic, sauté 1 minute, remove from heat.

Preheat oven to 400° F. Oil a deep baking pan to hold fish in a single layer.

Rinse and dry romaine. Dip in salted boiling water for 1 minute or less. Dry the leaves. Trim heavy stems. Overlap 2 leaves per fillet. Center fillet and sprinkle with leek and onion mixture. Completely wrap fish in romaine leaves, place in pan. Brush tops with oil. Add hot fish stock or water, red wine vinegar and bake about 12 minutes for small fish pieces, 15 minutes for larger fillets. Serve garnished with lemon slices and fresh mint leaves.

SEPHARDIC SWEET AVOCADO - Pareve

SERVES 8

3 ripe avocados

1/2 cup walnuts, ground

4 T orange juice

2 T lemon juice

2 T honey

1/2 tsp. cardamom

6 walnut halves

   orange slices, optional

Cut avocados in half, remove pits, scoop pulp into bowl. Mash avocado with a fork and stir in ground walnuts, orange and lemon juices. Add cardamom and honey, blend well. Chill and garnish with walnut halves and orange slices. Serve on lettuce leaves with matzo meal popovers.

SARDINE DIP - Pareve

MAKES 1 CUP

2 cans sardines in mustard sauce

4 green onions, chopped,
   reserve green tops

2 T matzo meal

   pepper to taste

1/2 tsp. horseradish, optional

Combine all ingredients in food processor until smooth. Garnish with green tops of onions thinly sliced and serve in a crock or spread on matzo crackers.

ROASTED GARLIC - Pareve

1 bulb garlic
1 T olive oil

Discard the heavier outer skins, separate the cloves or snip top of bulb. Arrange cloves in an oiled baking pan and brush cloves with oil. Roast at 350° F about 30 to 40 minutes. Roast a whole garlic bulb longer. Add selected herbs to flavor the garlic. (Roast several bulbs, they keep well).

Squeeze the soft garlic from the peel. Delicious on toasted matzo!

LEEK SPREAD ON MATZO - Pareve

2 cups water
1/2 tsp. salt
3 large leeks, discard dark green
2 T olive oil
salt and freshly ground pepper
1/4 cup vegetable stock **or** water
1 T roasted garlic, mashed
1 tsp. matzo cake meal
1/2 tsp. potato starch
1 tsp. fresh lemon juice
2 T unsalted Passover margarine
matzo or matzo crackers
4 T freshly snipped chives

Bring salted water to a boil. Slit leeks lengthwise, slice and cook partially covered until tender, about 10 minutes, drain. Rinse in cold water, drain well.

Heat olive oil in a heavy skillet on medium heat. Add leeks, salt and pepper, and sauté, turning to coat. Stir in vegetable stock, roasted garlic, cake meal, potato starch and lemon juice. Simmer until tender and thick. May be prepared ahead and chilled.

To serve, brush matzo squares with melted margarine and toast lightly under broiler. Spread leek mixture on matzo or Passover popovers, garnish with chives.

Option: ADD GRATED CHEESE AT A DAIRY MEAL.

FRESH GRATED HORSERADISH - Pareve

MAKES 1 QUART

12 oz or larger, horseradish root (reserve top for Seder plate)
1 medium beet, peeled and grated
2 T sugar
1 T kosher salt
3 T white vinegar

First my mother-in-law Becky Kekst; now our eldest son has this chore. It lasts until Rosh HaShanah!

Scrape and hand-grate horseradish root into a wide-mouth covered jar or grate in food processor. Place beet in small bowl, cover with ¼ C boiling water. Add salt, sugar and vinegar to horseradish root.

Cover jar and shake to blend well. Reserve ¼ cup for sauces. Add beet and liquid to jar, shake to combine thoroughly. Adjust taste with a bit more salt as desired. Store in a covered glass jar refrigerated. Watch your eyes.

TANGY TUNA SPREAD - Dairy

MAKES 1½ CUPS

- 1 can light tuna fish (6½ oz.)
- 3 T unflavored yogurt, drained
- 2 T mayonnaise
- 3 scallions, minced with green tops
- 1 tsp. prepared white horseradish, drained
- 1 tsp. lemon juice
  salt and pepper to taste
  minced parsley to garnish

Drain tuna. Process with remaining ingredients until smooth. Spoon in a bowl, cover and chill. Serve on matzo crackers or celery sticks, sprinkle with parsley.

OLIVE SPREAD - Pareve

MAKES 2 CUPS

- 1 can pitted black olives, drained
- 8 mint leaves, optional
- 1 clove fresh garlic
- 1 T roasted garlic
- 4 softened sun dried tomatoes, optional
- 1 to 2 T olive oil
- 2 T matzo meal
- 2 T parsley, minced

Process olives, mint, garlic and tomatoes until smooth. Add olive oil and pepper, process 15 seconds. Scoop into a small bowl, add enough matzo meal to make a cohesive mixture. Smooth top, garnish with parsley. Serve on matzo crackers.

STRAWBERRY BANANA SMOOTHIE-
Slushes for the kids - Pareve

MAKES 2 CUPS

- ½ cup strawberries
- ½ cup orange juice
- ½ banana
- ½ tsp. vanilla sugar
- ⅓ cup crushed pineapple, optional
- 2 T orange juice concentrate
- ½ cup ice cubes
- 2 fresh mint leaves, optional

Blend or process all ingredients until smooth. Try other fruits and vegetables.

LOW-FAT CHIVE CREAM CHEESE SPREAD - Dairy

MAKES 1 CUP

- 1 cup "yogurt cheese"
- 2 T minced scallions
- 2 T minced chives
- 2 T minced parsley
- 1/2 tsp. dried oregano, optional
- salt and pepper to taste

To make yogurt cheese, drain 3 cups yogurt overnight in the refrigerator. It yields approximately one cup yogurt cheese.

Add remaining ingredients, season to taste. Use as a dip for vegetables, spread on matzo or matzo meal bagels. Vary the herbs, use minced lox, jam or citrus juices to flavor cheese.

CHICKEN NUGGETS - Meat

6-8 CHILDREN'S PORTIONS

- 11/2 lb. boneless and skinless chicken breasts
- salt and pepper to taste
- 2 T matzo cake meal
- 1 egg white
- 4 T matzo meal
- 1/2 tsp. paprika
- vegetable oil **or** spray

Preheat oven to 400° F. Cut chicken into bite size pieces. Season with salt and pepper and dust with cake meal. Beat egg white with 1 tsp. vegetable oil. Dip chicken pieces into egg white then into matzo meal mixed with paprika.

Oil or spray a baking sheet and arrange chicken nuggets in a single layer. Spray the tops with vegetable oil spray. Bake 10 minutes, turn and bake 8 to 10 minutes more. Serve with purchased Passover barbecue sauce.

Note: PREPARE CHICKEN TENDERS THE SAME WAY FROM THE CHICKEN TENDERLOINS.

DRUMMETTES and WINGS- POLKES and FLIGELS - Meat

ABOUT 16 PIECES

- 2 lb. chicken drummettes and wings
- salt, pepper, and garlic powder
- 1 cup prepared Passover barbecue sauce

Season wings and drummettes with salt, pepper and garlic powder to taste. Marinate chilled in ½ cup sauce for 30 minutes. Broil under medium high heat, about 15 to 20 minutes, turning frequently. Dip into remaining sauce and keep warm. The kids love these.

FISH SALAD - *Pareve*

SERVES 8 TO 10 APPETIZER
PORTIONS

1	medium onion, sliced
1	stalk celery, sliced
4	sprigs parsley
1/2	tsp. salt and freshly ground white pepper
2	bay leaves
3	cups water
2	lb. large scrod fillets (**or** similar fish)
4	scallions, sliced including greens
1/4	cup each red, green and yellow pepper, chopped
4	T minced parsley leaves
3/4	cup 'lite' mayonnaise
1	tsp. white horseradish
	romaine lettuce leaves

Ideal as a Seder appetizer or with soup for a weekday lunch.

In a 3 qt. heavy bottomed pot, combine onion, celery, parsley, salt, pepper, bay leaves and water. Bring to a boil, simmer 5 minutes. Turn off heat, add fish fillets, cover, steep 10 minutes. Remove fillets to a bowl, cool to room temperature. Cut or break into one inch pieces.

Meanwhile finely chop scallions, the three colors of peppers and parsley. Combine with mayonnaise and horseradish. Reserve ½ cup sauce, pour remaining sauce over haddock pieces. Lightly toss to combine, including any poaching liquid that may have accumulated in bottom of bowl. Serve on romaine leaves. Add more horseradish to taste to reserved sauce, pass with fish salad. Serve with matzo crackers.

CHILLED SEA BASS MARINATED in LEMON and BASIL - Pareve

1/2	cup lemon juice, zest of one lemon removed in strips
3/4	cup white wine vinegar
1 1/2	tsp. salt
1/2	tsp. sugar
1	cup virgin olive oil
1/2	cup fresh basil leaves, chopped **plus** more for garnish
2	large garlic cloves, minced
1 to 2	tsp. dried hot red pepper flakes
2 1/2 to 3	lb. sea bass fillets, skinned, cut crosswise into 1 1/2" strips
1	cup dry white wine
2	bay leaves
2	parsley sprigs
1/2	cup chopped red bell pepper

Place lemon rind in a large shallow dish to hold fish in a single layer. In a medium bowl, whisk lemon juice, vinegar, 1/2 tsp. salt and sugar. Add oil in a steady stream whisking until marinade emulsifies. Add 1/4 cup chopped basil, garlic and red pepper flakes, reserve.

In a 6 qt. pot combine wine, bay leaves, parsley, remaining salt and 3 cups water. Bring to a boil, add sea bass and reduce to a simmer. Poach covered in batches for 4 minutes, until just firm to the touch. Remove with a slotted spoon to dish with lemon rind and pour the marinade over the sea bass. Marinate covered and chilled 8 hours or overnight.

Bring to room temperature one hour before serving. Arrange fish on serving plate, strain marinade into a small bowl. Whisk to emulsify and drizzle over fish. Garnish with remaining basil leaves and bell peppers. Use as an appetizer or a lunch dish.

Classic Chicken Soup with Mini Matzo Balls

SOUPS

"SMITE THAT ROCK, AND THERE SHALL COME WATER OUT IT, THAT THE PEOPLE

MAY DRINK." —**NUMBERS 11:5**

Chicken Broth with Vegetables Julienne

HOT SOUPS

CHICKEN STOCK - Meat

MAKES 6 QT. CHICKEN STOCK -
8 CUPS REDUCED SAUCE STOCK

- 5 lb. chicken backs, wings **or** turkey necks
- 5 lb. skinless chicken
- 6 large carrots, trimmed
- 2 large turnips
- 1 parsnip
- 5 stalks celery, trimmed
- 2 medium onions, peeled
- 3 bay leaves
- 2 strips lemon rind
- 8 sprigs parsley
- 8 whole white peppercorns
- 10 qt. cold water

Rinse and trim fat from chicken and bones. Place in a 16 qt. heavy stockpot over low to medium heat, toss to soften meat on bones slightly. Add chicken pieces and remaining ingredients. Bring to a boil, reduce heat, simmer about 3 hours, skimming occasionally. Strain stock into clean pot. Discard vegetables. Use chicken for other purpose.

Chill. Skim congealed fat. Add more vegetables (carrots, celery, bay leaves) and peppercorns. Return to heat, simmer to reduce by 25 percent. Salt after vegetables are tender. Use stock at this point to poach chicken or vegetables, to moisten kugels and stuffing. It is a rich broth, more concentrated than soup due to the large amount of bones.

Further reduced and blended with herbs, it coats chicken, turkey or veal with flavorful sauces. Reduce stock another 25 percent. When glossy and slightly thick, salt moderately as kosher chickens often need little salt. Freeze in 2 cup amounts in sandwich-size zip-lock bags. Be sure to get air bubbles out and close well. Defrost, add herbs.

PASSOVER NOODLES - Pareve

MAKES 2-2½ CUPS

- 4 large eggs **or** 3 eggs plus 1 white
- 4 T potato starch **plus** 1 T cake meal
- 1 cup water
- pinch of salt
- vegetable spray, oil **or** Passover margarine for frying

Beat all ingredients together, except oil. Oil fry pan, pour ¼ cup of batter into pan and immediately rotate. Cook until edges are dry and flip over for 30 seconds. Cool on a clean kitchen towel. Roll 5 pancakes together, plastic wrap, chill. Thinly slice rolls, drop in soup just to heat through. Handle these gently as they break easily; use similarly to pasta.

VEGETARIAN SOUP STOCK - Pareve -
Low Cholesterol

MAKES 8 QTS.

- 1 cup onion, chopped
- 2 garlic cloves, crushed
- 6 carrots, chopped
- 2 turnips, chopped
- 3 to 4 celery ribs, chopped
- 2 leeks, white only, rinsed and chopped
- 2 large potatoes, peeled and chopped
- 2 tomatoes, chopped, optional (omit for golden soup)
- 2 bay leaves
- 6 peppercorns
  left over mushroom pieces **or** vegetable trimmings
- 2 cups cabbage, shredded
- 1 scant tsp. kosher salt

Place all ingredients except salt in an 8 qt. heavy stockpot. Add 6 qt. water to cover vegetables. Add peppercorns and bring to a simmer. Cover, cook about 1½ hours, until vegetables are tender.

Strain broth, pressing out all liquid, discard vegetables or use elsewhere. Simmer stock to reduce by one fourth. Season with salt and pepper. Freeze or refrigerate until ready to use. Makes 4 qts. vegetarian stock.

MATZO BALLS - Meat

MAKES 18 LARGE MATZO BALLS

- 2 large eggs **plus** 3 egg whites
- 1¼ cups matzo meal
- 2¼ tsp. salt
- 2 T club soda
- 2 T chicken broth
- 4 T vegetable oil
- 1 T salt
- 2 T minced parsley **or** ¼ tsp. saffron, optional

Beat eggs and egg whites in a medium bowl with a pinch of salt. Stir in matzo meal, add salt, broth, club soda, oil, mix well. Chill 45 minutes. Bring an 8 qt. pot of salted water to boil. Moisten hands, make balls about the size of plums. Drop balls into pot and immediately cover. Keep at a rolling boil 45 minutes. Do not uncover, losing the steam will deflate matzo balls. Transfer to warm soup with a slotted spoon. Serve with parsley or saffron.

Option: CHILDREN LOVE MINI-MATZO BALLS. MAKE ABOUT 36 WALNUT-SIZE BALLS, BOIL ABOUT 30 MINUTES.

Matzo Ball Options: IN OUR HOUSE, YOU DON'T FUSS AROUND WITH MATZO BALLS. BUT I LOVE FLAVORED MATZO BALLS. THEY ARE DELICIOUS! TRY ¼ TSP. SAFFRON OR 1 T MINCED FEATHERY DILL. BOIL MATZO BALLS WITH 6 UNPEELED GARLIC CLOVES. BEST ARE STUFFED WITH CRISPED CARAMELIZED ONIONS, SINCE WE HAD TO GIVE UP GRIBENES STUFFED MATZO BALLS. MMMMM!

CLASSIC CHICKEN SOUP - Meat

MAKES 8 QTS.

one pullet, about 6 lb., remove skin and all fat

3 lb. extra breast bones, necks, wings or turkey necks

1 clove garlic, cracked

1 large onion, peeled and sliced

4 whole carrots, peeled

3 celery stalks

10-12 parsley stems

1 parsnip, peeled

3 bay leaves

5 or 6 white peppercorns

2 inch lemon peel, optional

9 qt. cold water

kosher salt and white pepper, to taste

Break extra chicken bones, cut up chicken and place in large stockpot over medium heat. Toss until meat on bones whitens, about 5 minutes. Add remaining ingredients, except salt. Slowly bring to a boil, skim occasionally. Simmer partially covered about 2 to 2½ hours. Remove chicken when tender for another use. Strain soup into cleaned pot, chill, remove all fat.

Return to a simmer, add fresh carrots. Reduce liquid slightly. Heat thoroughly, add salt and pepper to taste. Garnish with fresh parsley.

NUTRITIONAL ANALYSIS (with one Matzo Ball) per bowl

Total Calories: 371	Protein: 19 g (19%)	Sodium: 500 mg
Cholesterol: 71mg	Carbohydrate: 57g (59%)	Fiber: 7g
Fat: 10g (22%)	Alcohol: 0	

GOLDEN NOODLE SOUP - Pareve

YIELD: 10 CUPS

3 qt. clear vegetable stock

1/2 cup onions, diced

1 cup diced celery

1 cup sliced carrots

8 sprigs fresh thyme

2 bay leaves

1 cup sliced mushrooms

salt and freshly ground pepper to taste

1/4 tsp. saffron threads

1/4 cup finely minced parsley

2 generous cups Passover noodles

parsley sprigs

Bring broth to a boil in a heavy pot, add onions, celery, carrots, thyme, bay leaves, mushrooms, salt and pepper. Simmer vegetables gently until tender, about 20 to 30 minutes. Remove and discard bay leaves and thyme. Season to taste with salt and pepper, add saffron threads. Add noodles, heat on low until softened, do not boil; Passover noodles are delicate. Serve garnished with parsley. Keeps refrigerated 3 days.

FISH CHOWDER - Pareve

SERVES 8

1   T olive oil, **or** vegetable spray

1   cup each chopped leek, onions, carrots and celery

2 to 3   cloves garlic, minced

1/2   red pepper, chopped

1/2   yellow pepper, chopped

1   cup green beans, diced

    salt, pepper to taste, dash of cayenne

1   cup water

2   large potatoes, cubed

8   cups fish stock **or** gefilte fish "soup"

1 1/2   lb. firm fish filets, cut up **or** small fish pieces from the bones in the fish pot

2   T minced chives

When I make gefilte fish, this is a family favorite. Add latkes and gefilte fish samples for an easy supper on busy days before the Seders.

Heat oil in a 6 qt. pot, add leeks, onions, then garlic and sauté until soft. Add remaining chopped vegetables, sauté 5 minutes. Add water, bring to a boil, cover, simmer 10 minutes. Add potatoes, and strain fish stock through a fine sieve into the pot of vegetables. Season to taste with salt, pepper and continue to simmer until potatoes are tender. Add raw fish pieces, remove pot from heat, cover and set aside 10 minutes.

Add any other leftover cooked vegetables, mushrooms or cauliflower florets. Garnish with chives. Serve with gefilte fish samples and cheese latkes.

QUICK TOMATO SOUP - Dairy and Low Fat

MAKES 6 CUPS

2   T Passover margarine

2   leeks, white only

1 1/2   lb. fresh **or** one 28 oz. can whole tomatoes

2   medium potatoes, peeled and diced

1/2   tsp. sugar

3   cups water

    juice of half an orange

1   cup low-fat milk

    salt and freshly ground pepper to taste

    low fat sour cream, optional garnish

    minced parsley for garnish

Melt margarine in a 4 qt. pot and add leeks. Sauté until golden and limp. Add coarsely chopped tomatoes, cook until juicy. Add potatoes, sugar, salt and pepper. Add water, orange juice and cook until potatoes are very soft, about 25 minutes. Strain into a clean pot. Process solids until pureed.

Return puree to pot, add milk and heat gently. DO NOT BOIL. Serve with parsley and a dollop of low fat sour cream.

HOT BEET BORSCHT with FLANKEN -
Meat

SERVES 10 OR MORE

3	lb. lean flanken **or** boneless chuck
2	lb. or more marrow bones
4½	qt. cold water
1	medium onion
1	bay leaf
1	clove garlic
2	bunches beets, peeled
2	tsp. kosher salt, pepper to taste
¾	cup granulated sugar
1	scant tsp. sour salt **or** juice of one lemon
½	cup raisins

This was my Dad's absolute favorite. He ate huge bowls with matzo farfel.

Rinse bones in cold water, trim fat from meat. In a heavy pot combine meat, bones add cold water, slowly bring to a boil, skimming. Add onion, garlic, bay leaf, whole peeled beets, use some firm stems and crisp leaves. Cover, simmer 2 to 2½ hours, skimming occasionally, until meat and beets are tender.

Strain into clean pot. Discard all vegetables except whole beets. When beets are cool, grate into borscht pot. Skim fat. While warm, season with salt and pepper, sugar, sour salt, to taste. Often a bit more salt balances the sweet and sour flavors.

Cut meat into serving portions, return meat and bones to pot, add raisins, which will sweeten the borscht. Chill overnight to mature flavor; skim fat again.

Reheat, adjust flavors. Ladle into bowls with chunks of the meat, and marrow bones for the bone-lovers. Served with matzo farfel or matzo balls, it's a whole meal. Keeps 5 days.

Option: CHUCK OR TURKEY NECKS MINIMIZE FAT CONTENT.

ASPARAGUS SOUP - Dairy or Pareve

MAKES 8 CUPS

3	T unsalted Passover margarine **or** olive oil
1	cup mild white onion, diced
1	leek, sliced white only
2	medium potatoes
6	cups vegetable stock **or** water
10	sprigs parsley
15-20	asparagus trimmed, cut into 1" pieces, reserve tips
	salt, freshly ground pepper, to taste
1½	cups half and half **or** non-dairy creamer

Sauté onion and leek in melted margarine or olive oil in 4 qt. heavy stockpot. Cook 5 minutes, add asparagus chunks, cook another 2-3 minutes. Add peeled, diced potatoes, salt and vegetable stock or water, parsley and bring to a boil. Reduce heat, cover and simmer 30 minutes.

Meanwhile, gently steam or boil reserved asparagus tips. Refresh in cold water, drain and set aside. Strain soup into a clean pot, puree vegetables in processor or through a sieve. Return to pot, add half and half or non-dairy creamer. Adjust salt and pepper and heat thoroughly. Garnish with reserved tips.

ALBONDIGAS - GREEK MEATBALL SOUP

SERVES 8

2	carrots, sliced
2	leeks, white only, sliced
1	turnip, peeled and diced
4	tomatoes, peeled and chopped
	salt and freshly ground pepper to taste
1¹/₂ to 3	qt. water **or** vegetable stock
2	bay leaves
2	T Passover ketchup
	several dashes of ground cinnamon
6 to 8	red skin potatoes, par-boiled

Albondigas, a popular Sephardic main course, is similar to my grandmother's mid-Passover meal. I found it in the old English Jewish cookbook, THE JEWISH MANUAL by an English "Lady." It didn't include the dangerous New World vegetable, tomato, which I added.

Place all vegetables, except potatoes, in a large heavy 8 qt. soup pot. Add water or stock, bay leaves and bring to a simmer. Cook about 30 minutes, discard bay leaves. Season with salt and pepper to taste. Add ketchup and cinnamon, adjust flavor.

While soup cooks, make the **meatballs** (▶see page 88). Do not bake. Add potatoes to the bottom of pot, then drop meatballs on top. Rotate the pot to moisten meatballs. Cover and simmer 25 to 30 minutes.

Turn off heat, allow to sit 10 minutes. Ladle into deep soup bowls. A salad and Passover bagels make this a hearty meal.

TOMATO EGGPLANT SOUP with ROASTED PEPPERS - Pareve

SERVES 6 TO 8

2	medium eggplant, peeled, cut into 1" cubes
2	T fresh lemon juice
2	tsp. salt
1	each yellow and red bell pepper, peeled, cored and seeded
2	T olive oil
1	large onion, minced
2	garlic clove, minced
1¹/₂	lb. tomatoes, peeled, seeded and chopped
1	T chopped fresh thyme **or** 1 tsp. dried
	salt and freshly ground pepper, to taste
4	cups vegetable stock **or** bouillon
1	T chopped fresh parsley

Put eggplant in a colander and sprinkle with lemon juice and 2 tsp. salt. Toss and set aside for 30 minutes to drain. Meanwhile, roast peppers under broiler, turning until charred on all sides. Cover with a towel to cool slightly. Peel and set aside. In a large non-reactive pot, heat the olive oil on medium heat. Add onion and cook 3 minutes or until softened. Add garlic, cook 1 minute. Add tomatoes and thyme.

Rinse eggplant and pat dry, add to the pot. Season with salt and pepper. Cover and cook over medium heat, stirring 10 minutes until eggplant softens. Meanwhile, cut half the roasted peppers into small dice and set aside for garnish. Chop remaining peppers, add to the pot. Pour in the stock, bring to a boil. Reduce heat to a simmer, cover and cook 5 minutes. Strain. Puree solids in batches. Return to pot. Season with salt and pepper, stir in parsley and reheat. Serve garnished with the diced peppers.

NUTRITIONAL ANALYSIS (per serving):

Total Calories: 271	Fat: 11g (33.2% of calories from fat)	Protein: 8g
Carbohydrate: 40g	Cholesterol: 2mg	Sodium: 400mg

ROOT VEGETABLE SOUP - Pareve

SERVES 10

1   T olive oil

2   large leeks, sliced, white only

2   small onions, chopped

2   cloves garlic

2   medium purple skinned
    turnips, peeled and cubed

1   white turnip, peeled
    and cubed

2   parsnips, peeled and cubed

4   carrots, peeled and sliced

2   large baking potatoes,
    peeled and cubed

2   bay leaves, several sprigs
    of parsley and sage

4   peppercorns

8   oz. mushrooms, sliced

1   lb. small yellow or zucchini
    squash, thinly sliced

2   T tomato paste

    salt and pepper to taste

1/2 lb. fresh spinach leaves,
    trimmed

A hearty, healthy soup (Flavor with 1 cup dried beans after Passover)

Lightly oil a heavy 10 qt. stockpot over medium heat. Add leeks, sauté 5 minutes, add onions, sauté 5 minutes, add garlic. Add all turnips, parsnips, carrots and potatoes, cover with 4 quarts water. Add bay leaves, parsley, sage and several peppercorns. Cover and simmer 1½ hours, add water if necessary.

Discard bay leaves and sage sprigs. Add mushrooms, squash slices, tomato paste and cook 10 minutes. Season with salt and pepper to taste. Just before serving, add spinach leaves. Ladle a good mixture of vegetables into preheated bowls.

Serve with salad and matzo meal popovers for a hearty lunch.

NUTRITIONAL ANALYSIS

Total Calories: 128	Carbohydrate: 28g (84%)	Protein: 4g (12%)
Fat: 4 g	Cholesterol: 0mg	Fiber: 7g

POTATO, LEEK and PARSLEY SOUP - Meat

4 cups sliced white and pale green part of leeks (about 6)

4 T (1/2 stick) unsalted pareve margarine

1 white turnip, peeled and diced

3 lb. large boiling potatoes, peeled and diced

6 cups hearty chicken stock

1/2 tsp. kosher salt, freshly ground pepper to taste

1 cup non-dairy creamer, optional

1 cup fresh minced parsley leaves

long strands of chives

In heavy 6 qt. stockpot, sweat leeks in margarine, covered with a greased round of wax paper and the pot cover, over low heat. Stir occasionally for 30 minutes. Add turnip, potatoes, broth, 2 cups water, salt and pepper to taste.

Bring to a boil, simmer mixture 45 minutes uncovered, or until potatoes and turnips are tender. Cool 15 minutes. Strain the soup into a clean pot, puree the solids in batches, if necessary. Stir back into the liquid and simmer until thickened. Add parsley and optional non-dairy creamer for a very white soup. Simmer soup 5 minutes, do not boil. Garnish with long strands of chives across top of soup plates.

CARROT and GINGER SOUP - Meat

8 SERVINGS

2 T olive oil

2 lb. carrots, finely chopped

1 onion, medium, chopped

4 cups chicken stock

salt and freshly ground pepper to taste

one ginger piece, 2", peeled and minced

1 T potato starch

strands of chives to garnish

In a large 6 quart soup pot heat the oil, add the carrots and onion. Cook on medium high heat, stirring for 3 minutes or until the onion begins to soften. Pour in the broth, season with salt and pepper and bring to a boil on high heat. Reduce to a simmer, add ginger. Stir occasionally, cook about 20 minutes or until carrots are tender.

Strain and puree solids in a processor or blender until smooth. Stir the potato starch in 2 T cold water. Add to warm soup, slowly reheat, stirring until soup thickens slightly. Serve garnished with chive strands.

GARLIC and ALMOND SOUP - Dairy

MAKES 8 TO 9 CUPS

1/3 cup blanched almonds

3 large garlic bulbs, remove 2 large cloves, peel

2 T water

2 T olive oil

1 large onion, finely chopped

1 1/2 lb. potatoes, (Yukon Gold), peeled and diced

8 cups low sodium vegetable broth

salt and freshly ground white pepper to taste

1/2 cup plain nonfat yogurt (**or** non-dairy creamer **plus** 1/2 tsp. lemon juice)

2 T minced chives **or** parsley to garnish

Preheat oven to 400° F. Toast almonds on a cookie sheet or foil 4 to 5 minutes. Set aside.

Pull heavy skins from 3 heads of garlic, snip ends to expose. Reserve 2 large cloves. Place in foil, brush with 1 T olive oil, 2 T water and roast 30 to 45 minutes until very tender. Cool. Squeeze garlic flesh from skins, set aside.

Heat 1 T olive oil in a heavy 6 qt. soup pot on medium heat, add onion. Cook, stirring until browned, about 5 minutes. Crush and add the 2 reserved garlic cloves and potatoes. Cook, stir 2 minutes and add broth. Bring to a simmer. Reduce heat to low, cover and cook until potatoes are tender, about 20 minutes. Cool.

Strain soup into a clean pot, process solids with a little broth to a smooth puree. Whisk the puree into the broth. Puree roasted garlic heads and almonds until smooth, with a little soup. Whisk back into soup, season to taste with salt and pepper. Simmer to heat thoroughly. Serve hot with a dollop of yogurt and sprinkle with chives or parsley.

Note: FOR PAREVE SOUP, ADD 1/2 CUP NON-DAIRY CREAMER AND 1/2 TSP. LEMON JUICE FOR COLOR AND TEXTURE. SERVE WITH JERUSALEM ARTICHOKE SALAD.

NUTRITIONAL ANALYSIS

Total Calories: 210	Protein: 7g	Fat: 6g (0.7g saturated fat)
Carbohydrate: 30g	Sodium: 585g	Cholesterol: 5mg
Fiber: 2g		

COLD SOUPS

LOW CHOLESTEROL TANGY TOMATO SOUP - Pareve

MAKES 6 CUPS

- 1   46 oz. can unsalted tomato juice
- 1/4 cup lemon juice
- 1   tsp. sugar
- 1/4 tsp. garlic powder
       juice of half an orange
- 1   T grated orange rind
- 1/2 tsp. or more freshly ground pepper

Combine all ingredients in a 3 qt. microwave glass pitcher or bowl. Microwave on high 8 minutes, stir several times. Pour into mugs, sprinkle with freshly ground pepper. Serve hot or cold. Use as a cold refreshing drink. Serve with whole-wheat matzo crackers. Each ¾ cup has 38 calories.

CUCUMBER SOUP - Dairy

MAKES 8 CUPS

- 2   cups peeled and seeded cucumbers (about 4)
- 2   cups skim buttermilk
- 2   cups low fat sour cream
- 1/2 cup scallions
- 1/4 cup dill
- 1/4 cup parsley
- 3   T lemon juice
- 1   cup or more, water

Puree all ingredients in blender or processor. When smooth, pour into cups, garnish with cucumber spears. Serve chilled for lunch or snack. Serve with tuna fish salad for lunch. Makes 8 cups (2 grams fat per cup).

COLD BEET BORSCHT - Pareve or Dairy

YIELDS 12 CUPS

5 to 6   large beets, with stems and leaves

3   qt. water

1   tsp. salt

3/4   tsp. sour salt

1   tsp. lemon juice

several grinds freshly ground pepper

3/4   cup or more granulated sugar

low fat sour cream **or** plain yogurt to garnish

This Russian favorite is transplanted all over the world and very prominent in Israeli dairy restaurants. Serve clear or with the grated beets and cucumbers. My husband loves it as summer drink so we keep chilled pitchers.

Scrub beets, remove roots, green tops and stems. Trim rough area near beet tops. Wash well in cold water. Discard bruised stems. Cut large beets in half. In a 4 qt. heavy stockpot, combine beets, the firm stems, greens, water and ½ tsp. salt. Bring to a boil, cover and simmer about 30 minutes until beets are tender.

Remove pot from heat. Cool slightly and strain liquid into a clean pot, press juice from leaves and stems. When cool enough to handle, slip skins off beets, grate into clean pot. Stir in sour salt, lemon juice, pepper and sugar. Adjust flavor with a bit more salt or sugar as needed. If borscht is very strong, add a cup of ice cubes. Chill. Serve by the glassful with low fat sour cream, yogurt or diced cucumbers.

CHILLED ZUCCHINI SOUP - Dairy

MAKES 6 CUPS

2   T olive oil

1   medium onion, diced

6 to 8   small zucchini, sliced, reserve one for garnish

2   cloves garlic, minced

2   cups skim milk

1/4   cup parsley

1/2   tsp. dried thyme

2   cups milk

1   tsp. lemon juice

salt, fresh ground pepper

Heat oil in heavy pot over medium heat, add onion, sauté 3 to 4 minutes. Add zucchini and garlic, reduce heat to low, simmer covered until zucchini is very tender, 20 minutes. Remove, stir in 2 cups skim milk, parsley and the thyme, cool slightly.

Puree in batches in processor until smooth. Transfer to bowl, stir in remaining milk. Force through a sieve if a fine texture is desired. Add salt and pepper to taste. Chill.

Slice reserved zucchini into long thick strips and brush with lemon juice. Place one in each glass.

ISRAELI FRUIT SOUP - Pareve

SERVES 8

1   cup pitted chopped prunes

1/2 cup chopped dried **or**
     fresh apricots

2   qt. water

1   T lemon juice

2   cups fresh orange juice

1   piece 3" cinnamon stick

1/2 tsp. cardamom

2   whole cloves

1½   cups cored, peeled and
     chopped apples

1/2 cup golden raisins
     or currants

1   cup fresh orange segments

     pomegranate seeds,
     if available

Place prunes, apricots, water, lemon and orange juices in a non-corrosive 4 qt. pot. Add cinnamon, cardamom, cloves and bring to a simmer. Cover and cook gently 20 minutes.

Add apples and raisins, simmer 15 minutes more. Remove from heat, discard cinnamon and cloves. Chill in refrigerator several hours or overnight. Place in serving bowl or individual cups, garnish with orange segments and pomegranate seeds.

ICE COLD CAULIFLOWER SOUP - Dairy

MAKES 8 CUPS

1   large head cauliflower

1   cup water

     salt, pepper and a dash of
     cayenne pepper to taste

2   T Passover margarine

1   cup half and half

2   T sour cream

2   T chives, chopped

Trim heavy stalks close to the cauliflower florets. Steam over lightly salted water until very tender, about 25 minutes. Cool slightly, reserve some tiny florets to garnish. Process in batches until smooth with the cooking liquid. Add margarine, salt and pepper to taste.

Pour into a pitcher, add cream (or milk) and ½ cup of cooking liquid, chill thoroughly. Serve in mugs with a dollop of sour cream and chives.

BROCCOLI SOUP - Dairy

MAKES 8 CUPS

2¼ lb. fresh broccoli, rinsed

2 cups water

salt and pepper to taste

2 T unsalted butter
or Passover margarine

¼ cup finely chopped onion

1 T potato starch

1½ cups milk

½ cup cream (or milk)

4 T plain Yogurt

finely chopped chives
or scallion tops to garnish

Trim heavy ends of broccoli and remove waxy outer layer. Steam broccoli in vegetable steamer over boiling water until very green and tender, about 8 to 10 minutes. Rinse under cold water to stop cooking and retain color. Reserve 1 cup of the cooking liquid.

When cool, cut off flowerettes and stalks. Reserve ½ cup of tiny flowerettes. Puree remaining broccoli in batches in processor.

Melt margarine in 3 qt. heavy saucepan, stir in onion, sauté until softened, but not brown, about 3 minutes. Stir in potato starch, reduce to low, cook 2 minutes. Gradually stir in milk and cream. Cook until mixture thickens and nearly boils, 10 minutes. Reduce heat to low, stir in broccoli puree. Add reserved cooking liquid and reserved flowerettes. Serve hot or cold with a dollop of yogurt and chives.

CHILLED GAZPACHO SOUP - Pareve

SERVES 6

4 cups fresh tomatoes, peel, seed and chop, reserve juice

2 cloves garlic

1 medium onion

1 sweet red pepper

4 T cilantro

1 cucumber, peeled, seeded

salt and pepper to taste

2 tsp. lemon juice

2 tsp. horseradish, optional

Process garlic, onion, red pepper, cucumber, salt and pepper until lightly chunked. Remove ½ cup of vegetables, continue to process remaining vegetables until smooth. Season to taste with lemon juice, salt and pepper. Pour into a pitcher with the chunked vegetables. Adjust flavors. Chill.

Add more or less onions and garlic as desired. Contains no fat or cholesterol. Serve over ice filled glasses with celery or cucumber stalks to stir. Float slivers of horseradish on top.

STRAWBERRY RHUBARB SOUP - *Dairy*

3   cups (1 lb.) rhubarb,
cut in 1/2" pieces

3   cups water

1/2 cup sugar

1   tsp. grated orange peel

dashes of nutmeg

2   cups fresh strawberries,
rinsed and hulled

sour cream **or** yogurt,
optional garnish

mint leaves to garnish

In a large stainless steel pot, bring rhubarb, water, sugar and orange peel to a boil. Reduce heat and simmer 20 minutes. Puree in batches with 1 cup strawberries and nutmeg. Chill.

Serve with a dollop of sour cream or yogurt, sliced strawberries and a mint leaf.

Note: MAY BE FROZEN. THAW OVERNIGHT IN THE REFRIGERATOR.

ROOT VEGETABLE, APPLE AND PRUNE TSIMMES

POTATO KNISHES WITH CARMELIZED ONIONS

KUGELS
and CASSEROLES

"AND THEY BAKED UNLEAVENED CAKES OF THE DOUGH WHICH THEY BROUGHT

FORTH OUT OF EGYPT, FOR IT WAS NOT LEAVENED...NEITHER HAD THEY PREPARED

FOR THEMSELVES ANY VICTUAL" **EXODUS 12:39**

POTATO CHEESE CASSEROLE - Dairy

SERVES 6

- 3 medium baking potatoes, peeled, cubed
- 1 egg (or 2 egg whites)
- 1/4 cup low-fat Passover farmer's or ricotta cheese
- 1/2 cup skim milk
- 1 cup grated low fat Swiss cheese
- 3/4 tsp. salt, freshly ground pepper
- 1 tsp unsalted Passover margarine
- 1 1/2 T fresh thyme leaves, optional

Preheat oven to 350° F. Grease a deep 2 qt. casserole with margarine.

Boil potatoes in lightly salted water until just tender. Drain, cool slightly, press through a ricer or mash. In small bowl, whisk egg until smooth, add milk, farmer's cheese and 3/4 cup grated cheese. Stir into potatoes with salt, pepper and 1 T thyme leaves.

Spoon potato mixture into prepared casserole. Bake 30 minutes. Sprinkle with remaining cheese, bake 10 minutes. Sprinkle with remaining thyme.

CARROT APPLE and ALMOND KUGEL - Pareve - Low fat

SERVES 10 AS A SIDE DISH

- 2 T vegetable oil
- 1 lb. carrots, scraped and grated
- 2 tart apples, peeled and grated
- 1 T lemon juice
- 2 T orange juice
- 1 T sugar
- 3 cups matzo farfel
- 1 tsp. salt
- 1/2 tsp. ground ginger
- 1/4 tsp. grated nutmeg
- 1 tsp grated lemon zest
- 3/4 cup sliced almonds

Preheat oven to 350° F. Grease a 9 x 13" pan with 1 T vegetable oil.

Grate carrots and apples in food processor for a total of about 5 cups. Combine with lemon and orange juices in a large bowl.

Rinse matzo farfel in warm water, drain. Add farfel to carrot mixture with sugar, ginger, nutmeg, lemon zest, salt and 1 T vegetable oil. Taste and adjust flavor; batter should be moist. Spoon into prepared pan, scatter with almonds.

Bake 30 to 40 minutes until crisp on top and mixture is set. Serve hot or at room temperature.

SAVORY MATZO FARFEL KUGEL - Meat

SERVES 12

- 4   cups matzo farfel
- 2   small zucchini, grated
- 2   yellow squash, grated
- 2   medium carrots, grated
- 1   medium onion, grated
- 1   T roasted garlic
- 1   egg **plus** 2 egg whites, lightly beaten
-     kosher salt and pepper to taste
- 1   T dried sage leaves, crumbled
- 1½ cups chicken stock
- 2   T olive oil
- 6   medium leeks, white and light green only
- 1   clove garlic, crushed
- 4   T parsley leaves, chopped

Preheat oven to 375° F. Oil a 9 x 13" baking pan with 1T olive oil.

Soften matzo farfel in 1½ warm water, drain. Place in a large mixing bowl. Place grated squashes in a colander and lightly salt. Drain 15 minutes. Squeeze out excess moisture and add to the farfel with carrots, onion, roasted garlic, eggs and sage. Season to taste with salt and pepper. Stir in 1 cup rich chicken stock, adjust seasoning. Spoon into pan and cover with foil. Bake 45 minutes. Meanwhile prepare leeks.

Slice leeks lengthwise, rinse well. Cut crosswise in 1" pieces. Heat 1 T oil in a medium sauté pan. Sauté garlic and leeks, turning until very soft. Add remaining ½ cup chicken stock. Simmer until liquid is absorbed.

Uncover kugel, brush kugel with cooking liquid or a bit of oil, scatter leeks and parsley on top. (Can be made ahead to this phase.) Bake kugel 15 minutes more, until leeks are lightly browned. Cool 10 minutes, cut in 15 squares.

SWEET MATZO FARFEL and APPLE KUGEL - Pareve

SERVES 12

- 6   cups matzo farfel
- ½   cup golden raisins
- 1   T vegetable oil
- 4   oz Passover margarine, melted (1 stick)
- 4   eggs **or** 2 whole eggs and 2 whites, lightly beaten
- 3   tart apples, peeled, cored and grated
- 2   tsp. salt or to taste
- ¼   cup plus 1 T sugar
- 1½ tsp. cinnamon
- ½   cup slivered almonds **or** chopped walnuts, optional

Preheat oven to 350° F. Lightly grease a 9 x 13" ovenproof pan.

Soak farfel in 2 cups warm water 10 minutes. Drain in a colander, leaving farfel moist. Plump raisins in hot water 10 minutes. Mix margarine and eggs until thick. Add grated apples, sugar, salt, ¾ tsp. cinnamon and farfel. Add drained raisins. Taste mixture, adjust flavor. (As a dairy option, add 16 oz. low fat cottage cheese.)

Mixture should be loose. Spoon into prepared pan. Combine cinnamon with 1 T sugar and chopped walnuts. Sprinkle on top. Bake at 350° F, 40 to 45 minutes until golden. Cover if it browns too much. Cool 5 minutes before cutting into 15 squares.

APRICOT and PEAR KUGEL - Pareve

MAKES 15 SQUARES OR
12 SMALL KUGELS

- 6 cups matzo farfel
- 1 T vegetable oil
- 1 cup dried apricots, chopped
- 1/2 cup currants
- 1/2 cup white wine
- 4 slices matzo, toasted
- 4 oz Passover margarine, melted (1 stick)
- 4 eggs **or** 2 whole eggs and 2 whites, lightly beaten
- 1 pear, peeled, cored and grated
- 1 tsp. lemon juice
- 2 tsp. salt or to taste
- 2 T sugar
- 1 tsp. cinnamon
- 1/4 tsp. nutmeg
- 1/2 cup slivered almonds or chopped walnuts, optional

Preheat oven to 325° F. Grease a 9 by 13" ovenproof pan.

Soak farfel in 2 cups warm water 10 minutes. Drain in a colander, leaving farfel moist. Place in a large mixing bowl. Soak apricots and currants in 1/2 cup white wine, they should absorb most of the wine.

Toast matzo slices on a piece of foil in the oven for 10 minutes. Cool, rinse with warm water. Line the bottom of the pan with the slices and brush with oil or margarine.

Mix margarine and eggs until thick, stir into the farfel. Add grated pear, lemon, the apricot mixture and stir into the matzo farfel. Add salt, sugar, cinnamon, nutmeg and taste. Adjust flavors.

Increase oven to 350° F. Bake kugel 30 to 35 minutes. Brush top with melted margarine and sprinkle with almonds. Bake 10 minutes more. Cool briefly before cutting.

Option: BAKE THE FARFEL MIXTURE IN GREASED MUFFIN PANS FOR INDIVIDUAL LITTLE KUGELS.

EASIEST EVER TSIMMES - Pareve

SERVES 8

- 1/2 cup brown sugar
- 1 T potato starch
- 1/3 cup sherry or sweet red wine
- 1 can (20 oz.) pineapple chunks
- 3 T margarine
- 1/2 cup pitted prunes
- 2 cans (20 oz.) whole sweet potatoes
- 1/2 cup chopped pecans
- 1/2 cup golden raisins
- 1/4 cup dried currants

My sisters loved this really easy recipe.

Preheat oven to 325° F. Combine sugar, potato starch, sherry and juice from pineapple in a small saucepan. Simmer until thick, stirring constantly. Add margarine.

Arrange remaining ingredients in a 3 qt. casserole. Pour warm juice mixture over the top. Casserole may be covered with plastic wrap and refrigerated overnight. Bake 30 minutes. Do not overheat as all items are basically cooked. (Add another can of potatoes and 3 T of their liquid without any appreciable change.)

NUTRITIONAL ANALYSIS

Total Calories: 261	Fat: 3g	Carbohydrate: 50g	Sodium: 87mg
Cholesterol: 0	Protein: 3g	Protein: 3g	Alcohol: 0

POTATO and ZUCCHINI KUGEL - Pareve

SERVES 10

- 2 medium zucchini, grated
- 6 potatoes, peeled and grated
- 1 medium onion, grated
- 3 large eggs
  or 1 egg plus 3 whites
- 2 T matzo meal
- 1 tsp. potato starch
- 3 T vegetable oil
- 1 1/2 tsp. salt and 1/2 tsp. fresh ground pepper
  dash of sugar
- 2 tsp. dried marjoram
- 2 T chives, minced

Preheat oven to 375° F. Set out a 9 x 13" ovenproof pan.

Grate zucchini into a colander, lightly salt, drain 10 minutes. Meanwhile, grate potatoes, combine with eggs and grated onion. Rinse zucchini, drain well and add to potatoes with matzo meal, potato starch and 1 T oil. Mix well and season with a dash of sugar, marjoram, salt and pepper. Add a bit more matzo meal if needed.

Heat 2 T oil in pan for 3 minutes in oven. Pour potato mixture into the hot pan, bake 15 minutes. Reduce heat to 350° F, bake 15 to 20 minutes longer until golden. Scatter chives on top and cool before cutting.

THE POPULAR POTATO KUGEL - Pareve and Low-fat

SERVES 10

- 1 1/2 T vegetable oil
- 3 lb. baking potatoes, peeled and grated
- 1 medium onion, grated
- 4 large egg whites, lightly beaten
- 1/4 cup matzo meal
- 1 T potato starch
- 1 tsp. Passover baking powder, optional
  pinch of sugar
  salt and pepper to taste
  vegetable spray
  parsley leaves, minced

Preheat oven to 375° F. Grease a 9 by 13" pan with 1 tsp. oil.

Combine potatoes, onion, egg whites and 1 T oil. Stir in matzo meal, potato starch, baking powder, sugar, and salt and pepper to taste. Add a bit more matzo meal for a cohesive mixture.

Spoon into pan. Bake 15 minutes, spray or brush top with vegetable oil and sprinkle with parsley. Reduce heat to 350° F and continue to bake about 25 minutes until golden. Cool slightly. Cut into 15 squares.

PASSOVER POTATO KNISHES with
Caramelized Onions- Pareve

MAKES 8 KNISHES

vegetable oil **or**
cooking spray

1 heaping cup mashed
potatoes

1/3 cup matzo meal
or cake meal

4 T potato starch, divided

2 egg whites, lightly beaten

1/2 tsp. salt and 1/2 tsp. black
pepper

1 egg white

3 T matzo meal

1 cup caramelized onions
(▶see page 84)

2 T roasted garlic

Preheat oven to 375° F. Coat a baking sheet with vegetable spray.

In a bowl, combine mashed potatoes, matzo meal, 2 T potato starch, and egg whites. Knead together until firm. Season to taste with salt and pepper. Dust the counter and hands with potato starch. Divide dough into 8 or more balls. Flatten each into a disk.

Add garlic to prepared onions. Sauté half the onions in a sprayed small non-stick pan until crisp. Place 1 tsp. filling on each round. Fold over, moisten edges and press together firmly.

Brush knishes with a beaten egg white and press into matzo meal. Arrange knishes in a single layer and brush oil or spray top of knishes. Position baking sheet on bottom rack of oven. Bake about 15 minutes per side. Serve hot topped with remaining garlic and onions. Vary the fillings with other vegetables or meat.

Filling

Make filling as directed.

SPINACH GNOCCHI - Dairy

SERVES 6

2 pkg. frozen chopped
spinach, thawed and
drained

1 cup low fat Ricotta cheese

3/4 cup grated Parmesan cheese

1/4 cup potato starch

1 egg

1/4 tsp. grated nutmeg

1/2 tsp. salt, pepper, to taste

4 T matzo meal

3 T melted butter or
Passover margarine

minced parsley to garnish

Reserve 1/4 cup Parmesan cheese. Mix spinach with Ricotta, 1/2 cup Parmesan, the egg, potato starch, nutmeg, salt and pepper to taste. Add enough matzo meal to make a cohesive batter.

Boil 3 qt. of salted water. Sprinkle hands with potato starch to form batter into small balls. Carefully drop into boiling water in batches. When they rise to surface, remove with a slotted spoon to a bowl. Drain excess water.

Preheat oven to 325° F. Arrange gnocchi in a greased oven-proof dish in single layer. Drizzle with melted butter or margarine, 1/4 cup Parmesan cheese and bake 15 minutes. Serve hot.

SEPHARDIC SPINACH PIE - Pareve

MAKES 8 MAIN COURSE
PORTIONS

  4   T vegetable **or** olive oil

4 or 5 whole wheat **or** plain matzos

  2   lb. fresh spinach
       or 2 pkg. (10 oz.) frozen
       spinach, thawed and drained

  1   cup scallions, include half
       of green tops, chopped

  1   clove garlic, minced

      salt and pepper to taste

1/4 cup chopped fresh dill

1/2 tsp. cinnamon

3/4 cup matzo meal

  2   T potato starch

  6   egg whites, **plus** 3 yolks

  2   T lemon juice

  3   T pine nuts **or** pistachios

Preheat oven to 350° F. Lightly grease a deep, 10" pie plate.

Briefly rinse matzo sheets in water, drain. Fit matzo in bottom and sides of pie plate. Brush with oil.

Trim, wash, drain and chop fresh spinach. Heat remaining oil in a large skillet, sauté scallions until limp, add garlic, cook 2 minutes. Stir in chopped spinach, toss until wilted and coated with oil. Add salt, pepper, dill, cinnamon and ½ cup matzo meal mixed with potato starch. Adjust seasonings, set aside.

Beat egg yolks in a medium bowl with an electric mixer, add lemon juice, beat until thick and foamy, add to spinach mixture. Mixture should hold together. If needed, add more matzo meal.

In a clean large bowl of electric mixer with clean beaters, beat egg whites and a dash of salt until foamy, add a few drops of lemon juice. Beat until softly peaked. Fold into spinach mixture in two additions.

Spoon filling into prepared dish, brush top with oil. Bake 35 minutes, scatter nuts on top. Bake 10 minutes more until set and lightly browned. May be refrigerated overnight. Serve warm or at room temperature.

PERKY EGGPLANT CASSEROLE - Pareve

MAKES 6 CUPS

  2   lbs. eggplant

  2   T olive oil

  1   medium onion, chopped

  2   cloves garlic, minced

  1   can plum tomatoes (14 oz.),
      chopped, reserve juice

      juice of 1/2 a lemon

  1   tsp. sugar

1/2 cup coriander
      or parsley, chopped

1/2 tsp. cumin, optional

      salt and pepper to taste

  1   tsp. each, basil and
      oregano

1/2 cup pitted black **or** green
      olives

Preheat oven to 450° F. Prick eggplant several times with fork. Place on baking sheet, bake until soft and a bit collapsed, about 35 to 45 minutes. Turn once or twice. Cool. Peel, discard skin and seeds, chop.

In a large, heavy saucepan, heat oil on medium heat. Sauté onion until golden, 5 minutes. Add garlic, sauté 2 minutes. Add eggplant, tomatoes, lemon juice, and sugar. Add coriander or parsley, salt and pepper and cumin. Simmer 10 minutes more, stir in basil and oregano. Add reserved tomato juice as needed. Garnish with olives. May be made one day ahead. Serve at room temperature spread on matzo or as a side dish.

A PASSOVER LASAGNA - Dairy

MAKES 9 PIECES

- 2   T vegetable oil
- 6   whole matzo slices
- 1 3/4 cup tomato juice
- 1/4   cup catsup
- 1   garlic clove crushed
- 1   T sugar
- 2   T chopped parsley
-      salt and pepper to taste
- 1   tsp. each, fresh oregano and basil
- 1   small onion, grated
- 1   egg, well beaten
- 8   oz. low fat cottage cheese
- 8   oz. Swiss cheese
- 3   oz. grated Parmesan cheese

Preheat oven to 350° F. Oil a 9" square baking pan. Pour hot water over matzo in a colander, drain immediately. Dry on wax paper.

Combine tomato juice, garlic, catsup, sugar, parsley, salt, pepper, oregano, basil, oil and onion. In another bowl, combine egg, cottage cheese and grated Swiss cheese.

Spoon 1/3 of the sauce into pan, fit a layer of matzo over sauce into corners, spread half the cheese mixture. Repeat layer ending with matzo. Top with sauce and grated Parmesan. Bake 45 minutes. Cool 10 minutes, cut in squares.

NUTRITIONAL ANALYSIS

Total Calories: 71	Fat: 1g	Carbohydrate: 13g	Sodium: 355mg
Cholesterol: 0	Protein: 1g	Fiber: 4g	Alcohol: 0

PASSOVER POTATO DUMPLINGS - Pareve

MAKES 18 DUMPLINGS

- 1   bulb roasted garlic, (▶see page 11)
- 2   T olive oil
- 4   large potatoes
- 1/4   cup oil
- 4   eggs, beaten
- 1/2   tsp. kosher salt, pepper to taste
- 4   T potato starch
- 2 to 3 T matzo meal

Preheat oven to 325° F. Cook potatoes in salted water until very soft. Drain, mash by hand, not in a processor. Add oil, eggs, salt and pepper. Add potato starch and enough matzo meal for a soft, cohesive batter. Chill one hour.

Dust work surface with more potato starch, press potatoes into a 12" square, 1/2" thick. Bring a 6 qt. pot of salted water and 1 T olive oil to a boil. Dust hands with potato starch. Cut potato batter into about 18 squares or form balls, drop into boiling water in batches, cook about 5 minutes. They float to the top when cooked. Remove with a slotted spoon to bowl.

Drain accumulated cooking water from bowl. Coat dumplings with 1 T olive oil, salt and pepper. Break roasted garlic apart and scatter on dumplings. Serve as a side dish or in chicken broth with the sweet garlic cloves.

Option: USE THIS SAME RECIPE AND POUR THE POTATO BATTER OVER THE TSIMMES. ROAST COVERED 30 MINUTES. UNCOVER, BASTE WITH TSIMMES JUICES TO BROWN.

ROOT VEGETABLE, APPLE and PRUNE TSIMMES - Pareve

SERVES 12

- 4 large yams, peeled and cut into cubes
- 1 medium butternut squash, peeled and cut into cubes
- 3 large baking potatoes, peeled and cut into cubes
- 3 carrots, peeled, sliced 1/2"
- 1 turnip, peeled and diced
- 2 cups water
- 1 tsp. potato starch
- 3/4 cup sweet red Passover wine
- 3 green apples, peeled, cored and diced
- 1 cup pitted prunes
- 1/4 cup raisins
- 4 T honey
- 1 T lemon juice **and** 2 tsp. grated lemon zest
- 3/4 tsp. salt
- 1/2 cup pecans, optional

Preheat oven to 425° F.

Toss carrots, potatoes, squash and turnip in a deep, heavy 10 x 15" baking pan, add 2 cups water. Cover with foil, bake 15 minutes, reduce oven to 350° F and roast 30 minutes. Baste occasionally.

Dissolve potato starch in the wine, add to pan juices. Add apples, raisins, prunes, honey, lemon juice and zest, salt and stir well. Cook 20 to 30 minutes more. Adjust flavor to taste slightly sweet and sour. Prepare ahead to this point.

Reheat covered at 325° F. Uncover pan to evaporate juices and thicken.

NUTRITIONAL ANALYSIS

Total Calories: 265   Protein: 3g   Carbohydrate: 55g   Fat: 4g
Alcohol: 2g   Cholesterol: 0

QUICK PASSOVER PIZZA - Dairy

SERVES 6

- 2 eggs (1 egg plus white is okay)
- 1/2 cup milk
  salt and pepper to taste
- 6 squares matzo
- 6 slices American cheese
- 1 can Passover tomato mushroom sauce
  dried basil **or** oregano to taste
- 1/4 cup Parmesan
- 1 T Passover margarine to grease pan

Preheat oven to 375° F. Lightly grease a baking sheet.

Beat eggs and milk with salt. Dip matzo slices into mixture, soak 5 minutes. Lift to baking sheet and arrange cheese slices over matzo. Spoon sauce on top. Sprinkle with desired herbs and Parmesan cheese. Bake 10 to 15 minutes. Rest a few minutes before cutting into squares. Serve immediately.

MATZO BREI (MATZO FRY) - Pareve

SERVES 2

4   sheets matzo, broken up

3-4 T vegetable oil

    salt and pepper to taste

3   T water

    pinch of sugar, optional

2   whole eggs
    plus 1 or 2 egg whites

1   T melted Passover margarine

Plain and fancy, it's a great favorite!

❖ ❖ ❖

Moisten matzo, toss with 2 T oil and 3 T water, season with salt and pepper. Lightly beat whole eggs and egg whites until softly peaked, add to matzo mixture. Heat 1 T oil in a heavy 11" skillet. Spoon in mixture, flatten and cook 3 to 4 minutes. Add a bit more oil, flip matzo fry to brown other side, cook 2 to 3 minutes. Serve immediately with sugar, jam, yogurt or fruits.

Note: THE MORE EGG, THE FLUFFIER!

Variations:

- Stir mixture to cook similarly to scrambled eggs.
- Add sautéed or crisp onions, mushrooms or diced salami (meat).
- Sauté apple slices in margarine and brown sugar for a topping.
- Add sautéed sliced leeks, green peppers and minced parsley.

PASSOVER MOCHERAI MIX - Pareve

MAKES 8 CUPS

8   matzo, various flavors, broken-up

1/2 cup shredded carrots

1/2 cup multi-colored Passover fruit cereal

3   small apples, cored, quartered and thinly sliced

1   tsp. cinnamon

3/4 cup warm orange juice

1   T oil

1/4 cup honey

4   T apple juice concentrate

1/2 cup chopped nuts

8   oz. dried mixed fruits, cut up

Great snacks for the kids.

❖ ❖ ❖

Preheat oven to 275° F.

Place broken matzo in a large bowl. Toss with cereal, carrots, apples and cinnamon.

In a small bowl, combine warm orange juice, oil, honey and apple juice concentrate. Stir to blend honey. Drizzle over matzo mixture and mix well. Let stand a few minutes to absorb the liquid. Mix again.

Spread the mixture onto two nonstick baking sheets, bake 2 hours, stirring every 30 minutes. It will be very moist after the first 30 minutes. Add almonds during last 20 minutes of baking. Cool, transfer to a large bowl, mix in the dried fruit. Store in an airtight container.

ZUCCHINI PIZZA - Dairy

SERVES 8

- 4 cup shredded zucchini
- 2 T matzo meal
- 1 egg **plus** 1 egg white, lightly beaten
- 2 tsp. dried oregano, crushed
- 1 tsp. dried basil, crushed
- 2 cup shredded mozzarella
- 2 cup shredded cheddar cheese
- 1 medium onion, minced
- 1 T Passover margarine **plus** 1 T olive oil
- 1 can 14 oz. tomato sauce
- 1 green pepper, cut in thin strips
- 8 oz. mushrooms, sliced
- 2 cloves garlic
- 1/2 cup Parmesan cheese, grated

  salt, pepper, garlic powder to taste

Good all year round.

Preheat oven to 400° F. Lightly oil a 10 x 15" jelly roll pan.

Sprinkle zucchini with salt, drain in colander 10 minutes. Rinse, press out excess moisture. Place in a bowl, add matzo meal and beaten eggs. Stir in oregano, basil, 1 cup mozzarella and 1 cup cheddar, season to taste with salt and pepper. Press an even layer of zucchini mixture into pan. Bake 10 minutes.

Meanwhile, sauté onions and garlic in margarine until limp. Add tomato sauce, simmer 10 minutes.

Spoon tomato sauce on baked zucchini, arrange vegetables on top, season with salt, pepper and garlic powder. Sprinkle with remaining cheeses, ending with Parmesan cheese. Bake 25 to 30 minutes until top is crisp and bubbly. Cool briefly. Serve cut into squares. Try other vegetables.

PASSOVER GRILLED CHEESE "SANDWICHES" - Dairy

MAKES 8 "SANDWICHES"

- 4 slices matzo
- 8 slices Passover American cheese
- 2 eggs **plus** 1 egg white
- 3 T milk

  salt and pepper to taste

  Passover margarine for frying

Donna Yanowitz makes these for her grandchildren's lunches.

Briefly rinse matzo in warm water, place on wax paper. Cut matzo in quarters and fit cheese slices on half the quarters. Top with remaining matzo.

Beat eggs with milk, salt and pepper to taste. Place one matzo sandwich in the egg mixture, turn after one minute. Heat 2 T margarine in an 11" non-stick sauté pan. Sauté sandwiches quickly in batches, until golden. Transfer to a greased 9 x 13" ovenproof pan. Make 2 hours ahead to this point.

Preheat oven to 350° F. Bake 10 minutes until hot and bubbly.

CHREMSLACH-CHEESE PANCAKES - Dairy

MAKES 16 PANCAKES.

- 4 eggs (or 2 whole eggs and 3 whites)
- 2 tsp. vanilla sugar
- 8 oz. ricotta cheese
- 3 T butter or Passover margarine, melted
- 1/2 tsp. salt, dash of pepper
- 1/2 cup matzo meal

  several dashes ground nutmeg
- 1/4 cup softened raisins, optional

  vegetable oil **or** margarine for frying

  syrup, recipe follows

Beat eggs and a pinch of salt until foamy, add vanilla sugar, beat until light in color. Add cheese, melted butter or margarine, salt, and stir in matzo meal to make a cohesive mixture. Add nutmeg and raisins.

Heat oil in a large fry pan, drop batter by tablespoons, flatten with back of moistened spoon. Fry in batches, about 3 minutes per side, until golden. Drain on a paper towel lined platter. Serve with syrup, jam, sour cream or cinnamon sugar.

Variations:

- **PERKY PANCAKES** eliminate sugar, raisins, nutmeg. Add 1/4 cup thinly sliced scallions and 2 T chives, salt and pepper.
- **APPLE PANCAKES** Grate an apple into batter, serve with applesauce.
- Add 1/2 cup Parmesan cheese to plain batter, serve with tomato mushroom sauce.
- **VEGETABLE PANCAKES** Sauté 1 cup minced vegetables add to batter.

PASSOVER SYRUPS

1 CUP

- 3/4 cup honey
- 3 T water
- 2 T lemon juice

Honey Syrup

Simmer all ingredients 1 hour. Strain through a sieve. Keep warm.

3 CUPS

- 1 lb. dark raisins, plumped
- 6 cups water
- 1 T lemon juice

Raisin Syrup

Simmer raisins covered in hot water about 1 hour. Add lemon juice, simmer until very thick.

PASSOVER CHOLENT - Meat

SERVES 8

- 6 whole baking potatoes
- 2 whole sweet potatoes
- 2 onions, quartered
- 3 carrots, cut in chunks
- 4 to 5 lbs. brisket
- 1 large apple, peeled and sliced
  salt and pepper to taste
- 1 T cinnamon
- 2 cups apple juice
- 1/2 tsp. ground ginger
  water to cover

Peel potatoes and place in a deep stockpot or crockpot. Add onions, carrots and place brisket on top. Season to taste with salt, pepper and cinnamon. Add juice and water to cover. Bring to a simmer on top of the stove. Add apple and ginger. Place in a 250° F oven. Cook overnight, basting occasionally. Add water and seasoning as needed.

Option: USE A WHOLE CAPON INSTEAD OF BRISKET.

VEGETARIAN TSIMMES - Pareve

SERVES 8

- 2 lb. carrots
- 3 lb. sweet potatoes
- 2 lb. white potatoes
- 1 small onion, minced
- 1 apple, peeled and chunked
- 1 cup pitted prunes
- 4 T honey
- 4 T brown sugar
- 2 tsp. grated lemon zest
- 1 T lemon juice
- 1 tsp. salt and 1/4 tsp. pepper
- 2 cups water
  marjoram **or** sage leaves to garnish

Peel carrots, slice 1 inch thick; peel and chunk all potatoes. Preheat oven to 425° F.

Toss carrots, potatoes, onion and apple in water in a deep, heavy 10" x 15" baking pan. Cover, reduce heat to 375° and roast 30 minutes, shaking pan occasionally.

Add prunes, honey, brown sugar, lemon zest, juice, salt and stir well. Cook 20 to 30 minutes more, taste and adjust flavor. Juices should taste slightly sweet and sour. Uncover to evaporate juices and thicken slightly. May be made one day ahead.

Bring to room temperature and reheat covered at 325° F. Vegetables should be very tender. Garnish with fresh herbs.

Pale Green Spring Salad

Middle East Roasted Tomatoes

VEGETABLES
and SALADS

"And they came to Elim, where were twelve springs of water and three score and ten palm trees..." —Exodus 15:27

Honey Glazed Carrots

VEGETABLES

BAKED APPLE and SQUASH SLICES -
Pareve

SERVES 8

2 medium acorn or butternut
 squash, peeled, seeded and
 sliced 1" thick

3 T Passover brandy
 or white wine

1/2 tsp salt, to taste

 "lite" olive oil
 plus vegetable oil spray

3 tart apples, peeled, cored
 and sliced 1/2" thick

 juice of 1/2 lemon

4 T brown sugar

2 T Passover margarine

 several grinds of nutmeg

 cranberry sauce, optional

A tasty Tsimmes alternative.

Preheat oven to 425° F. Generously spray a 10 x 15 x 2"
ovenproof pan with vegetable spray.

Sprinkle squash with brandy or wine and oil. Place squash
rings in a single layer if possible, lightly salt. Bake about 20
minutes, turn once and continue baking. Pare and slice
apples, coat with lemon juice

When squash is nearly soft, add apple slices. Bake 10 to 15
minutes, sprinkle with brown sugar, nutmeg and dot with
margarine. Bake until just tender. Dot with cranberry
sauce.

NUTRITIONAL ANALYSIS

| Total Calories: 197 | Fat: 4g | Carbohydrate: 31g | Sodium: 87mg |
| Cholesterol: 0 | Protein: 1g | Fiber: 6g | Alcohol: 12% |

SWEET and SOUR ARTICHOKES - Pareve

MAKES 8 PORTIONS

2 pkg. frozen artichoke hearts

1/3 cup apple juice

 juice and zest of one lemon

2 to 3 T honey

 pinch of salt

1/4 cup snipped chives

Cut artichokes in bite-size pieces. In a 3 qt. saucepan, simmer with apple juice, lemon zest and juice, honey and salt,
covered for 10 minutes. Uncover, simmer to evaporate
most of the juices. Sprinkle with chives. Serve at room
temperature.

NUTRITIONAL ANALYSIS

| Total Calories: 48 | Fat: .9g | Carbohydrate: 11 g | Sodium: 11g |
| Cholesterol: 0 | Protein: 1g | Fiber: 2g | Alcohol: 0 |

FRIED ARTICHOKES, ITALIAN STYLE -
Pareve

SERVES 12 AS A SIDE DISH

- 12 small tender artichokes, tips and stems trimmed
- 2 lemons, juice and rinds
- 2 T salt
  and 1 tsp. fresh ground black pepper
- olive oil for deep frying

Trim long strips of zest from lemons, reserve. Place artichokes in large bowl of water with juice of 2 lemons until ready to cook. Hold 2 artichokes at a time over the bowl and tap against each other to drain and open leaves. Season all over with salt and pepper.

Heat oil on moderate heat in a deep pot. Stand artichokes in a single layer, cook 20 to 25 minutes. Bottoms and sides should be browned. Sprinkle artichoke tops with cold water occasionally to steam during cooking. Remove, stand on a platter. May be prepared to this point several hours ahead.

To serve, reheat oil. Lift artichokes with a fork inserted in bottom. One at a time dip in hot oil. Leaves open like a flower. Serve warm or at room temperature.

ROASTED ASPARAGUS with SWEET PEPPER CONFETTI - Pareve

SERVES 6

- 1 lb. fresh asparagus, or more
- 1/2 tsp. kosher salt
- 2 garlic cloves, minced
- 2 T olive oil
- 1/4 cup each yellow, red and orange pepper, diced

Everyone's favorite.

Preheat oven to 475° F. Line a baking sheet with foil, set aside.

Rinse, trim asparagus and pat dry. Spread asparagus on a baking sheet in a single layer. Drizzle with olive oil, salt, and garlic, toss to coat well. Keep at room temperature 15 minutes. Roast 5 minutes. Turn asparagus, add diced peppers and cook 2 minutes more. Serve immediately or at room temperature. There's never enough!

NUTRTIONAL ANALYSIS

| Total Calories: 44 | Fat: 2g | Carbohydrate: 6g | Sodium: 269 mg |
| Cholesterol: 0 | Protein: 3g | Fiber: 3g | Alcohol: 0 |

BRAISED ARTICHOKES and GARLIC - Dairy

SERVES 8 AS A SIDE DISH

- 4 medium artichokes
  juice of one lemon
- 1 head garlic
  salt and pepper to taste
  sprigs of feathery dill
- 4 T feta **or** dry farmer's cheese

Trim heavy stem and outer leaves. Cut sharp points from top of artichokes. Place artichokes in water with juice of half a lemon.

Cut tips of garlic cloves, separate from base, drop into boiling water for about 30 seconds, drain. When cool enough to handle, peel.

In an 8 qt. stockpot, simmer 2" of water. Add 2 dill sprigs, remaining lemon juice, salt and pepper and cook one minute. Add artichokes cut side down. Cover, cook 20 minutes, add garlic cloves. Simmer 10 to 15 minutes, until tender.

With a large fork, lift artichokes to platter, spread leaves, remove choke and scatter garlic on top. Adjust flavor of cooking liquid, simmer to reduce slightly. Strain onto plates to dip leaves. Garnish with dill. Serve at room temperature with a sauce or feta cheese. (The garlic is sweet as sugar.)

Dill Sauce

Mix ingredients together. Pass with artichokes.

MAKES 1 CUP

- 1 onion, chopped
- 1 cup mayonnaise
- 2 T chopped dill
  salt, pepper, paprika
  dash of sugar

Horseradish Sauce

Mix ingredients together. Pass with artichokes, fish or vegetables.

MAKES 1½ CUPS

- 8 oz. whipped cream cheese
- ¼ cup white horseradish
- 1 T sugar
- ½ tsp. salt
- 1 cup cream

ROASTED BEETS and ONIONS - Pareve

MAKES 2 CUPS

2	lbs. beets
1	lb. small red pearl onions
2	T olive oil
	salt and pepper to taste
3 or 4	slivers of horseradish
2	T chives, snipped

Preheat oven to 375° F. Cut two pieces of foil and brush with olive oil.

Scrub and trim beets. Cut large beets in half. Lightly oil beets, arrange in a single layer on foil and enclose securely. Set the packet on a baking sheet, roast 35 minutes.

Meanwhile, blanch onions 5 minutes in boiling water, rinse in cold water. Remove skins and enclose onions in another oiled sheet of foil. Roast onions and beets another 20 minutes.

When vegetables are tender, open packets and cool. Slip off beet skins and toss with onions in a bowl. Season with salt and pepper. Can be made two days ahead and chilled. Garnish with horseradish and chives. Use as a relish.

SWEET and SOUR CANDIED BEETS - Pareve

MAKES ABOUT 3 CUPS

4	cups coarsely shredded raw beets
2 1/2	cups sugar
2	small oranges, remove peel and segment skin
1	large lemon, thinly sliced
1/2	cup water
1	tsp ground ginger
1/2	tsp. salt
1/2	cup chopped walnuts, toasted
1/2	cup dried cranberries

Place all ingredients except nuts and cranberries in a 6 qt., heavy, non-corrosive pot. Slowly bring to a simmer. Cook, stirring occasionally for about one hour. Add small amount of water as needed.

Beets should be jellied and glossy. Add dried cranberries. Store chilled in a 1 qt. glass jar. Garnish with walnuts. Serve with turkey or beef.

HONEY GLAZED CARROTS - Pareve

SERVES 6 SIDE-DISH PORTIONS

1¼ lb. Belgium carrots, whole
   or slivered lengthwise

4 T fresh orange juice, strained

1 T lemon juice

1 tsp. Passover margarine

½ tsp. salt

1 tsp. grated orange zest

1 tsp. grated lemon zest

1 tsp. fresh grated ginger

6 T honey

Fresh dill sprigs to garnish

Combine carrots, juices, margarine and salt in a 2 qt. saucepan. Cover and simmer about 10 to 15 minutes until just tender. Remove from heat, stir in zests, ginger and honey. Serve warm or at room temperature garnished with dill sprigs.

BAKED CARROT RING - Pareve

SERVES 10

2 T unsalted pareve margarine

4 cups thinly sliced carrots

1 small whole onion

   salt and freshly ground
   black pepper to taste

1 tsp. cinnamon
   and 1 tsp ground ginger,
   a pinch of cloves

4 eggs, separated
   or 2 whole eggs and
   4 whites

½ cup sugar

¼ cup matzo meal

1 cup ground walnuts

Preheat oven to 350° F. Grease a 2½ qt. ring mold with 1 T margarine.

In a 2 qt. saucepan, cook carrots, onion, a dash of salt in enough boiling water to cover. Simmer until carrots are tender, about 20 minutes. Discard onion, drain carrots and puree. Spoon into a bowl, add remaining margarine, cinnamon, ginger, cloves, ¼ tsp. salt and pepper to taste.

Beat egg yolks and ¼ cup sugar until thick and pale, stir into carrot mixture and margarine. Beat whites until foamy, gradually increase speed, slowly add remaining sugar, beat until stiff but not dry. Fold into carrot mixture alternately with matzo meal and nuts. Mixture should light. Turn into prepared mold. Set mold in larger pan of boiling water in lower third of oven. Bake 45 minutes until set. Cool 10 minutes. Unmold on serving platter.

NUTRITIONAL ANALYSIS

| Total Calories: 96 | Fat: <1g | Carbohydrate: 18g | Sodium: 205mg |
| Cholesterol: 0 | Protein: <1g | Fiber : 2g | Alcohol: 0 |

FRIED SEPHARDIC EGGPLANT SLICES -
Dairy

SERVES 8 AS A SIDE DISH
OR APPETIZER

1¹/2 lb. small eggplants (about 3)
  2 tsp. kosher salt, pepper
     to taste
1¹/2 cups milk
  2 egg whites, lightly beaten
¹/8 tsp ground cardamom
¹/4 cup matzo cake meal
     vegetable oil for frying
  2 T parsley chopped
  4 T Parmesan cheese, grated

Preheat oven to 300° F.

Peel eggplant and slice ½" thick. Sprinkle with 1 tsp. kosher salt, place in colander to drain 30 minutes. Rinse, place in bowl, cover with milk (or an egg white) to draw out salt. Heat 1½" oil in a 10" deep fry pan or pot to medium high.

Drain eggplant, pat dry, season with salt, pepper and cardamom. In batches, dip eggplant slices in egg whites, then cake meal, shake off excess, drop into hot oil and fry about 3 minutes per side until golden. Drain on paper towels. Place fried slices on a baking pan. Sprinkle with parsley and Parmesan. Heat to melt cheese.

GINGERED TOMATO AVOCADO RELISH -
Pareve

MAKES 1¹/2 CUPS

  1 navel orange
  2 large tomatoes, chopped
  2 avocados, peeled and diced
  4 green onions, trimmed
     and chopped
  2 T olive oil
  1 T lemon juice
  1 T sugar
  1 tsp. minced fresh ginger
     salt and pepper to taste
  2 T fresh parsley, chopped

Cut orange in half, remove and chop the pulp, reserve shells. Combine tomatoes, avocados, onions and orange pulp in a medium bowl. Mix together olive oil, lemon juice and sugar. Pour over vegetables, stir in ginger, season to taste with salt and pepper. Refrigerate several hours.

Spoon into reserved orange shells and garnish with parsley.

MIDDLE EAST ROASTED TOMATOES -
Pareve

SERVES 12 AS A SIDE DISH

12	Italian plum tomatoes cut in half
3	cloves garlic, minced
	salt and pepper to taste
1/4	cup olive oil
1	T lime juice
1	tsp. dried rosemary

Preheat oven to 350° F.

Salt tomato halves and turn upside down to drain for 15 minutes. Oil a large non-corrosive baking pan to hold the tomatoes in a single layer. Sprinkle tomatoes with garlic. Season to taste with salt and pepper. Mix olive oil, lime juice and rosemary together. Brush on tomatoes. Bake about 30 minutes until tomatoes are soft but retain their shape.

Serve warm or at room temperature.

WILD MUSHROOM PATE - Pareve

MAKES 2 CUPS

1/3	cup minced shallots
4	T unsalted Passover margarine
1	lb. assorted mushrooms, shiitake, portobello, cremini, oyster
1	tsp. dried rosemary **or** thyme
1/4	cup red wine
1/2	cup pareve mushroom broth from bouillon cube
2	T matzo meal
	rosemary or thyme sprigs

In a large skillet, cook the shallots in the margarine over medium heat, stirring occasionally until softened. Add mushrooms, herbs and cook stirring until all the mushroom liquid evaporates. Add the wine, and simmer until it is nearly evaporated. Add broth and simmer until reduced by half.

Transfer to a food processor and puree until smooth. Add 1 to 2 T matzo meal to make a cohesive mixture. Season to taste with salt and pepper. Transfer to a bowl or crock. Chill several hours. Garnish with fresh herb sprigs and serve on matzo crackers or celery stalks.

STEAMED BRUSSELS SPROUTS- Pareve

SERVES 6

1 1/2	lb. fresh Brussels sprouts
1	tsp. lemon juice
1	T olive oil
	salt and pepper to taste
1/2	cup chestnuts, optional

Cut an "X" in the bottom of each sprout and remove hard outer leaves. Place in 2 qt. pot fitted with a steamer. Add 1/2 cup water and a dash of salt. Cook about 12 to 15 minutes until tender and bright green. Drain and lift sprouts to a bowl. Toss with lemon juice, olive oil, salt and pepper to taste. Garnish with chestnuts.

Note: REMOVE ALL LEAVES FROM THE BASE AND STEAM THE LEAVES FOR 5 MINUTES. BRUSSELS SPROUTS TASTE ENTIRELY DIFFERENT.

ROASTED CAULIFLOWER with ONION AND ROSEMARY - Pareve

MAKES 8 CUPS

- 2 heads cauliflower, about 2 lbs. separated into 1" flowerettes
- 2 medium red onions, cut into 12 wedges
- 4 cloves garlic, peeled and crushed
- 2 T olive oil
- 3/4 tsp. salt
- 1/4 tsp. coarsely ground black pepper
- 1/4 cup fresh parsley leaves, chopped
- 1 T fresh rosemary leaves

  rosemary sprigs for garnish

Our daughter-in-law makes this delicious version for our family.

Preheat oven to 450° F. Lightly oil two 10 x 15" baking pans.

In a large bowl, toss all ingredients except parsley and rosemary sprig until evenly mixed. Divide mixture onto the pans. Season to taste with salt and pepper.

Roast vegetables about 40 minutes or until tender and lightly browned. Stir occasionally and rotate pans halfway through cooking. Transfer to serving platter, sprinkle with parsley and garnish with rosemary sprig. Serve warm or at room temperature. (Can be made ahead and refrigerated overnight.)

A CONFETTI of MEDITERRANEAN VEGETABLES - Pareve

SERVES 8

- 1 1/2 lb. zucchini, scrubbed, cut into julienne strips
- 1 1/2 lb. summer squash, cut into julienne strips
- 1/2 cup white onion, chopped
- 1/2 cup red onion, chopped
- 3 carrots, peeled, cut into julienne strips
- 1/4 tsp. grated nutmeg
- 1/2 tsp. cinnamon **mixed** with a dash of sugar

  salt and pepper to taste
- 3 T olive oil
- 2 T lime juice

  coriander **or** mint leaves to garnish

In a colander, toss the squashes with salt, drain 30 minutes. Rinse, pat dry and place in a large bowl with remaining vegetables. Combine seasonings, oil, lime juice, and toss with vegetables. Keep covered at room temperature one hour. May be chilled overnight. Adjust flavor. Garnish with coriander or mint. Serve at room temperature.

VEGETABLE PATTIES - Pareve

MAKES 12 PATTIES

- 1 cup minced red pepper
- 1/2 cup minced green peppers
- 2 T olive oil or vegetable spray
- 1 1/2 cups grated carrots
- 1/3 cup grated onion
- 1 garlic clove, minced
- 1 lb. raw spinach, trimmed and chopped (2 cups)
- 2 cups cooked potatoes, mashed
- 1 egg **and** 3 egg whites, beaten
- 1 tsp salt, 1/2 tsp pepper
- 1 T unsalted Passover margarine, melted
- 1/2 cup matzo meal
- 2 T matzo cake meal
- vegetable oil **or** spray for frying

Sauté peppers in 1 T olive oil about 10 minutes, until limp. Add carrots, grated onion, garlic and sauté until tender, about 10 minutes. Add spinach and potatoes, cook 2 minutes. Remove to a bowl, cool slightly. Add eggs, salt and pepper to taste, matzo meal and 1 T melted margarine. Let thicken about 30 minutes.

Preheat oven to 350° F.

Form 3" patties, dust with matzo cake meal. Fry in a light film of oil or vegetable spray in a non-stick pan, about 4 minutes per side. (Can be made several hours in advance.) Place on a non-stick cookie sheet and bake about 15 minutes to get a bit crisp. Serve with applesauce or sour cream. A delicious lunch.

EGGPLANT SPREAD - Pareve

MAKES 2-2 1/2 CUPS

- 2 lb. medium eggplants
- 1 large onion, chopped
- 3 to 4 cloves garlic, minced
- 1 small green pepper, seeded and chopped
- 1/4 cup parsley
- 1/4 cup olive oil **or** mayonnaise
- 3 T vinegar
- dash of sugar, salt and pepper to taste
- 2 T matzo meal

Heat oven to 350° F. Cut a slit in each eggplant, place on a baking sheet and bake until very tender, about 40 minutes. Cool. Peel eggplant, mash pulp and add remaining ingredients. Spread mixture on a plate. Let sit at room temperature 30 minutes to mature flavor. Serve with matzo crackers or use to dip a variety of colorful fresh sliced peppers, celery and carrots.

BAKED PUREE of CELERY ROOT and PEARS - Pareve

SERVES 8

6 T lemon juice

6 T water

4 large nearly ripe pears

2 lb. celery root, peeled, cut into 1" dice

1/2 cup pareve chicken bouillon

salt and pepper to taste

2 T sugar

1/2 tsp. cardamom

4 T pareve margarine

2 tsp. chopped Italian parsley

Preheat oven to 375° F. Mix lemon juice and water in medium bowl. Peel, core and cut pears into 8 pieces each. Place in lemon water. Add diced celery root to lemon water and toss well. With a slotted spoon, lift pears and celery root to a shallow baking dish. Add ¼ cup of remaining lemon water and the chicken bouillon. Stir in salt, pepper, sugar and cardamom. Mix well. Dot vegetables with margarine, cover and bake 1½ hours.

Stir twice while baking. Process with the pan juices until smooth. If mixture is stiff, add a bit more chicken bouillon. Spoon into shallow casserole, brown under broiler briefly. Serve warm, garnished with parsley.

BRAISED RED CABBAGE WEDGES - Pareve

SERVES 8

1 2/3 lb. red cabbage

1 large tomato, peeled, seeded and chopped

1/3 cup dry red wine

1 1/2 T chopped red onion

2 T chopped red bell pepper

4 T Passover margarine

1 1/2 tsp. red currant jelly

1/8 tsp. sweet paprika

1/4 tsp. salt

1/4 cup crumbled matzo farfel

Trim and discard stem and tough leaves of cabbage. Rinse, cut cabbage in half lengthwise. Cut and discard core. Slice each half into 3 wedges. Rinse and drain on paper towels.

Combine tomato, wine, onion and bell pepper in blender or processor. Puree until smooth, scrape down sides as needed. Heat 3 T margarine in a 12" skillet on medium heat. Add tomato mixture, bring to a boil. Blend in jelly, paprika and salt, simmer 30 seconds to blend flavors, stir constantly. Add a bit of water if needed. Arrange cabbage wedges in skillet, turn to coat well. Cover, reduce heat to medium low. Cook about 15 minutes, until thickest part of cabbage is tender, basting frequently.

Meanwhile melt remaining 1 T margarine in a medium skillet on medium high heat, add matzo farfel and stir until golden brown and slightly crisp. Sprinkle farfel on a serving tray. Remove cabbage with a slotted spoon, drain excess liquid and arrange over the farfel on a heatproof platter. Keep warm in low oven. Heat braising liquid over medium heat to reduce to ¼ cup. Spoon over cabbage.

SCALLION CASSEROLE - Dairy

SERVES 8

- 8 bunches green onions, cut crosswise into 1" pieces
- 2 cloves garlic, minced
- 3 T unsalted butter or Passover margarine
- 1/4 cup heavy cream
- 1/2 cup Parmesan cheese, freshly grated
- 1 T olive oil
- 1 1/2 cups matzo meal
- 3 T minced chives

Preheat oven to 350° F. Grease a 1½ qt. shallow casserole. In an 11" sauté pan, heat the butter or margarine and cook scallions and garlic until limp, about 20 minutes. Stir in the cream and ¼ cup Parmesan cheese. Spoon into casserole.

In same pan, heat olive oil on medium high heat, add matzo meal, stir until golden, about 3 minutes. Transfer to a bowl, cool slightly. Add remaining Parmesan cheese, season with salt and pepper. Spread crumb mixture over scallions, top with chives.

Bake uncovered for 20 to 25 minutes. Serve warm or at room temperature.

"SCHNIPPLED" GREEN BEANS - Dairy

12 PORTIONS

- 2 lb. green or yellow string beans or combination
- 1 medium onion, peeled and thinly sliced
  salt and fresh ground pepper to taste
- 1 tsp. sugar
- 1 tsp. white wine vinegar
- 3/4 cup reduced fat sour cream
- 1 T fresh thyme **or** mint leaves

Trim and cut green beans on an angle into two-inch pieces. Slice onion, lightly salt and set aside to drain 15 minutes. In a 2 qt. pan, simmer enough salted water to cover beans. Slowly add beans so boiling is constant. Boil 4 to 5 minutes until beans reach their height of color. Immediately plunge into ice water to stop the cooking. Drain and pat dry. Place in serving bowl. Can be made one day ahead.

Note: FROZEN BEANS PURCHASED BEFORE PASSOVER MAY BE USED

Add onions to bowl of beans. Combine ingredients for dressing, toss with beans about 15 minutes before serving. Serve at room temperature or very cold.

WHIPPED SWEET POTATO GRATINEE -
Pareve

SERVES 6

3 lb. about 6 medium sweet potatoes

1 T vegetable oil

4 T Passover margarine

1/2 tsp. salt

3 T frozen orange juice concentrate

1 T grated orange zest

4 T Passover pancake syrup **or** brown sugar

Scrub potatoes, rub skins with vegetable oil. Place on foil and bake in 425° F oven until tender, about 40 minutes. (Can be done in the microwave). Slice potatoes in half when cool enough to handle, scoop filling into large bowl.

Add 3 T margarine, orange juice and salt. Beat with hand mixer until well combined. Grease a 2 qt. ovenproof casserole with remaining margarine. Spoon in potato mixture, making grooves with a fork. Drizzle with syrup or brown sugar and sprinkle with orange zest. Can be prepared one day ahead to this point. Heat 25 minutes in a 375° F oven to heat thoroughly and lightly brown on top.

WHIPPED POTATOES with CRISPY ONIONS - Pareve

SERVES 8

4 to 5 lb. Yukon Gold potatoes peeled and sliced

6 T unsalted Passover margarine

salt and pepper to taste

1/2 cup non-dairy creamer

2 T **roasted garlic puree** (▶see page 11)

1 cup **caramelized onions** (▶see page 84)

In a 6 qt. heavy pot bring 4 qt. of salted water to a boil. Add potatoes and boil about 20 minutes, until tender, drain. Return pot of potatoes to warm burner, toss to evaporate moisture. Mash with a potato masher or whip with a hand mixer on low. Add 4 T margarine, non-dairy creamer and roasted garlic. Season to taste with salt and pepper.

Preheat oven to 375° F. Melt remaining 2 T margarine and grease a 3 qt. casserole. Transfer potatoes to casserole, brush top with remaining margarine and add onions. Bake for 25 minutes until onions are crisp.

SPINACH SOUFFLÉ - Pareve

SERVES 8

2 T soup mandlen, ground

2 1/2 T Passover margarine

2 pkg. (10 oz.) frozen chopped spinach

1 tsp lemon juice

3/4 T potato starch

2 whole eggs, **plus** 1 egg white, separated

1/2 cup mayonnaise

1 tsp. ground nutmeg

1/2 tsp. salt, fresh ground pepper to taste

dill sprigs

Preheat oven to 350° F. Grease a 1 qt. soufflé dish with 1/2 T margarine and dust with 1 T mandlen crumbs. Cook spinach in a sauté pan until moisture is released. Reserve 3/4 cup of cooking liquid and drain remaining spinach.

In processor with metal blade, puree spinach and lemon juice 15 seconds, set aside. Melt 2 T margarine in a 1 qt. saucepan, add potato starch and slowly add reserved spinach liquid, stirring constantly until smooth. Remove from heat, cool slightly. Beat in 1 egg yolk.

In processor bowl, beat remaining egg and egg whites. Blend in mayonnaise, nutmeg, salt and pepper. With machine running, pour in potato starch mixture, blend 30 seconds. Add to chopped spinach, mix well. Taste, adjust seasoning, pour into prepared soufflé dish. Sprinkle remaining mandlen on top.

Bake 40 to 50 minutes until lightly browned and well puffed. Serve immediately. If served a bit later, soufflé will collapse slightly, but tastes fine at room temperature. Garnish with dill.

GLAZED CELERY ROOT and CARROTS

6 SERVINGS

1 large celery root, cut into 1/4 inch slices

1 lb. carrots, sliced

1/2 cup chicken stock or water

3 T lemon juice

2 T brown sugar

salt and pepper

mint leaves or coriander

Simmer celery root, carrots, chicken stock or water, lemon juice and brown sugar about 30 minutes. Season to taste with salt and pepper. Uncover to reduce juices about 3 minutes. Juices will glaze the vegetables. Garnish with coriander or mint leaves.

SALADS

ARUGULA and ORANGE SALAD - Pareve

SERVES 6

1/4 tsp. crushed green peppercorns

    zest of a navel orange, peel segments

1 bunch arugula

1 small bunch endive

1 head Boston, Romaine **or** other lettuce

4 T olive oil

1 cup fresh orange juice

    salt and freshly ground black pepper, to taste

1 T Passover white wine vinegar

1/2 cup thin red onion slices

    fresh coriander **or** parsley

Drain orange sections, reserve juice. In small bowl, toss oranges with peppercorns, set aside.

Wash arugula, endive and lettuce, drain and tear in bite size pieces, place in salad bowl. In a small bowl, whisk olive oil with salt, vinegar and olive oil, add orange juice and orange zest. Pour over greens, toss and divide on plates. Top with oranges and onions.

NUTRITIOANAL ANALYSIS

Total Calories: 322	Fat: 21g	Carbohydrate: 25g	Sodium: 99mg
Cholesterol: 0mg	Protein: 11g	Fiber:6g	Alcohol:

GARLICKY TOMATO SALAD - Pareve

SERVES 8

6 tomatoes

6 chopped garlic cloves, or more

1 T fresh parsley, chopped

2 T olive oil

1 T red wine vinegar

    salt and 1/2 tsp. black pepper

1 tsp. fresh basil, chopped

    coriander sprigs to garnish

Use the delicious Israeli tomatoes cut in half or thickly slice local tomatoes. Arrange on serving dish. Sprinkle with parsley. Whisk together olive oil, vinegar, salt, pepper and basil. Pour over tomatoes. Marinate 30 minutes or more. Garnish with coriander.

SWEET ONION SLAW - Pareve

SERVES 6

- 1/2 cup apple juice
- 2 large sweet onions, Maui or Vidalia, sliced
- 1 large red onion, sliced
- 1 egg or white only
- 4 tsp. cider vinegar
- salt and ground pepper to taste
- 3/4 cup olive oil
- 2 tsp. sugar
- 1/3 cup finely chopped scallions
- 1/3 cup finely chopped parsley

Bring apple juice to a boil in large non-corrosive saucepan. Turn off heat, add onions, toss to coat, cover and let stand 30 minutes.

Process egg, 1 tsp. cider vinegar and salt until blended. Activate machine, slowly add oil until mixture thickens, season with remaining vinegar, sugar, salt and pepper to taste.

Drain onions, place in serving bowl, add dressing with scallions and parsley. Flavor improves overnight.

CHICKEN, PEPPER and ONION SALAD - Meat

SERVES 6

- 2 cups cooked chicken
- 6 small red-skinned potatoes, cooked, optional
- 1/2 cup each red, green and yellow bell peppers, coarsely chopped
- 1/2 cup red onion, chopped
- 1 cup celery, sliced
- salt and freshly ground pepper
- 1/2 tsp. cumin
- 1/2 tsp. curry
- 1 can mandarin oranges, drained

Here's something tasty to do with the soup chicken!

Cut chicken and potatoes into bite-size pieces. Combine with peppers, onion, celery, salt, pepper, cumin and curry. Adjust seasonings and set aside.

MAKES 1/2 CUP

- 1/2 cup mayonnaise
- 1 tsp. horseradish
- 1 T lime juice

Dressing

Combine dressing ingredients. Stir into salad and adjust seasoning. Garnish with oranges.

MIDDLE EAST TOMATO and CUCUMBER SALAD - Pareve

SERVES 8

4 firm ripe tomatoes, skins and seeds removed

2 seedless English cucumbers, peeled, seeds removed

5 T olive oil

juice of one lime

2 garlic cloves, peeled and crushed

1/2 tsp. kosher salt, 1/4 tsp. fresh ground pepper

3 scallions, chopped

5 radishes sliced

1 cup chopped fresh parsley

1/3 cup fresh chopped mint

dashes of nutmeg

In a bowl, cut tomatoes and cucumbers into 1" cubes. In a large bowl, whisk together olive oil, lime juice, garlic, salt and pepper. Toss tomatoes, cucumbers and remaining vegetables and herbs. Serve immediately.

"CHAROSET" SALAD - Pareve

SERVES 8

5 to 6 tart apples, cored and diced

2 T pineapple juice

1 T sweet white wine

1/2 cup celery, chopped

1/4 cup dates, chopped

1/4 cup raisins

1 cup walnuts chopped

1/2 tsp. cinnamon

3/4 cup mayonnaise

Toss apples with pineapple juice and white wine in a bowl. Add remaining ingredients, mix well. Cover with plastic wrap, chill.

Serve on lettuce leaves. Add chunks of leftover or "soup" chicken for a quick, hearty lunch salad.

Note: COOKED, DICED MEAT MAY BE ADDED TO THIS SALAD.

PALE GREEN SPRING SALAD - Pareve

2   tart green apples, core
    and thinly slice

    juice of 2 limes,
    grated zest of one lime

2   cans artichoke hearts,
    drained and chopped

6   scallions, sliced

2   large cucumbers, sliced
    lengthwise, peel, seed
    and cut crosswise

2   stalks celery hearts,
    thinly sliced

8   pitted green olives, sliced

    salt and freshly ground
    white pepper

1   tsp. horseradish grated

2   T light olive oil

4   T cilantro or parsley, minced

2   peeled avocados, sliced

1   cup seedless green grapes

Coat sliced apples in a large bowl with lime juice to prevent discoloring. Add lime juice and zest, artichoke hearts, scallions, cucumbers, celery hearts, green olives, salt and pepper and horseradish. Coat well with olive oil, cover and chill 1 hour. To serve, coat avocado slices with lemon or lime juice or the lime vinaigrette. Arrange over salad with the grapes and sprinkle with cilantro. Pass dressing.

NUTRITIONAL ANALYSIS (excludes dressing)

Total Calories: 103	Fat: 4 g	Carbohydrate: 16g	Sodium: 136mg
Cholesterol: 0mg	Protein: 3g	Fiber: 5g	Alcohol: 0

MAKES 1 CUP

2   T water

1/4   cup lime juice

1/2   cup olive oil

2   T white wine vinegar

    salt and white pepper
    to taste

1   small garlic clove, minced

1   T minced scallions

Lime Vinaigrette

Combine all ingredients in a jar, mix well. Pass with salad separately.

CUCUMBERS and TOMATOES in YOGURT
- Dairy

SERVES 8

3/4 lb. cucumbers, seeded,
    cut in 1/2" dice

1/2 lb. fresh ripe plum tomatoes,
    seeded, cut into 1/2" dice

4   fresh mint leaves, chopped

2   T lemon juice

    salt and fresh ground
    pepper to taste

1/2 cup plain yogurt

    sprigs of dill and mint
    to garnish

Combine diced vegetables in a medium bowl, toss with remaining ingredients, stir in yogurt and chill several hours. Adjust seasonings. Add radishes or other vegetables as desired. Garnish with dill and mint leaves.

ISRAELI CARROT SALAD - Pareve

SERVES 6

1   lb. fresh young carrots

1   T orange zest

1/2 cup fresh orange juice

1   tsp. lemon juice

    pinch of sugar

1/2 cup golden raisins, optional

    several grinds of nutmeg

Scrape and grate carrots into medium bowl. Toss with orange juice and zest, lemon juice and sugar. Add raisins and allow to mature at room temperature. Toss occasionally. Serve as side side salad.

BEET and APPLE SALAD - Pareve

- 2 lb. beets, fresh cooked **or** canned, sliced julienne
- 1 medium red onion, chopped
- 1/2 cup vegetable **or** walnut oil
- 2 T red wine vinegar
- 1 T lemon juice
- salt and pepper to taste
- pinch of sugar
- 2 tart green apples, cored and coarsely chopped
- 1/4 cup pecan pieces
- salad greens
- whole wheat matzo

Combine beets and onions in a bowl. Whisk together oil, vinegar, lemon juice, salt and pepper, a pinch of sugar. Pour over beet mixture, toss well. Taste, add more sugar if tart. Often a bit more salt brings flavors together. Cover and allow to marinate 3 hours.

Mix in apples and place on a bed of greens. Garnish with pecans, serve with whole wheat matzo.

▲ STUFFED BREAST OF VEAL, (recipe on page 108)
MIDDLE EAST ROASTED TOMATOES, (recipe on page 54)
ROASTED BEETS AND ONIONS, (recipe on page 51)
AND ROASTED ASPARAGUS WITH SWEET PEPPER CONFETTI (recipe on page 49)

▲ FESTIVE SWEET BRISKET WITH FRUIT (recipe on page 100)

▶ **top right** BONELESS STUFFED BREAST OF VEAL (recipe on page 108)

▶ **bottom right** PASSOVER POTATO KNISHES WITH CARMELIZED ONIONS (recipe on page 38)

▲ HAND-PAINTED MATZO COVER FROM ISRAEL

◀ RASPBERRY POACHED PEARS (recipe on page 142)

▼ BROWNIE PIE (recipe on page 137)
AND APPLE NUT RING (recipe on page 145)

▲ Chicken Broth with Vegetables Julienne (recipe on page 18)

◄ **top left** Pale Green Spring Salad (recipe on page 64)

◄ **bottom left** Braised Chicken Thighs and Drumsticks (recipe on page 87)

▲ HALIBUT WRAPPED IN ROMAINE (recipe on page 10)

▶ **top right** TURKEY SCHNITZEL WITH CRANBERRY SAUCE (recipe on page 96)

▶ **bottom right** CLASSIC CHICKEN SOUP (recipe on page 20)
WITH MINI MATZO BALLS (recipe on page 19)

▲ Medley of Sorbet, (recipe on page 147)
Orange Slices with Moroccan Spices
(recipe on page 141)

◄ far left Chocolate Elegance with Chocolate
Mousse (recipe on page 121 and 122)
and the Versatile Jelly Roll with Apricot Filling
(recipe on page 118)

◄ A Contemporary Israeli Kiddush Cup used as
Elijah's Cup

▲ A Passover Pavlova (recipe on page 132) with Strawberry Sauce (recipe on page 141)

◀ **top left** Elegant Stuffed Peppers, (recipe on page 114)
Schnippled Green Beans, (recipe on page 58)
and Sweet and Sour Artichokes (recipe on page 48)

◀ **bottom left** Crusted Turkey Loaf with Gingered Tomato Avocado Relish (recipe on page 53)

▲ ROOT VEGETABLE, APPLE AND PRUNE TSIMMES, (recipe on page 41)
SPINACH MOUSSAKA, (recipe on page 112)
AND DRUMMETTES AND WINGS - POLKES AND FLIGELS (recipe on page 13)

Brisket of Beef with Fruit Sauce

Crusted Turkey Loaf with Tomato Ginger Sauce

MAIN COURSES

"Take an unblemished lamb from your flock...eat the flesh in that night, roast with fire and unleavened bread; with bitter herbs they shall eat it...in the morning, none shall be left. And thus shall ye eat it...with your shoes on and your staff in your hand; ye shall eat it in haste— it is the Lord's passover." **Exodus 12:5-11**

"And it came to pass at even, quails came up...." **Exodus 14:13**

While the Israelites ate their meal in haste, we are privileged to eat our sumptuous Passover feast in leisure. Busy homemakers need only hasten to complete the extensive Seder food preparations. Main courses partially or fully prepared in advance, ease a cook's chores. Consider the Seder's numerous fish and matzo ball soup courses when calculating main course amounts. It's helpful to be able to freeze leftovers.

Spinach Moussaka

FISH

SALMON CAKES with CARAMELIZED ONIONS - Dairy

> 3 lb. white onions, thinly sliced
> 2 T olive oil
> dash of salt and a dash of sugar

The Onions

Heat oil in 6 quart heavy-bottomed pot. Sauté onions with a dash of salt until limp. Add sugar, reduce heat to medium low and continue cooking up to 45 minutes. Stir occasionally. Onions will be a rich golden color. About 3 cups cooked onions are needed. Meanwhile prepare salmon cakes.

SERVES 8 AS AN APPETIZER,
4 AS A MAIN COURSE

> 1½ lb. cooked fresh salmon **or** 2 - 16 oz. good quality salmon
> ½ to 1 cup toasted matzo meal
> ⅓ cup low fat milk
> ¼ cup mayonnaise
> 2 T parsley
> 1 egg lightly beaten
> 2 T tomato paste
> ½ tsp. salt
> ¼ tsp. freshly ground white pepper
> 3 cups caramelized onions, 2 cups roughly chopped
> 2 T vegetable oil plus 2 T unsalted Passover margarine **or** vegetable cooking spray
> ¼ cup matzo cake meal
> 1 tsp. paprika
> fresh parsley sprigs

The Salmon Cakes

Place boned, flaked salmon in a large bowl, cover with ½ cup toasted matzo meal. Pour milk over matzo meal to moisten. Combine ¼ cup mayonnaise, egg, parsley, tomato paste, 2 cups chopped onions, salt and pepper in a small bowl. Combine with fish mixture.

Form salmon cakes, into 2½ inch rounds. Heat oil and margarine in a 10" skillet over medium heat. Combine matzo cake meal and paprika, lightly dust on salmon cakes. Fry until golden brown, 3 to 4 minutes per side. Garnish each salmon cake with a heaping spoon of warm caramelized onions and a sprig of parsley. Serve hot or at room temperature.

NUTRITIONAL ANALYSIS

Total Calories: 176
Fat: 6g
Carbohydrate: 20g (80%)

Cholesterol: 21mg
Protein: 11g (16%)
Alcohol: (0%)

ESCALOPE of SALMON and GINGER - Pareve

8 APPETIZER OR 4 MAIN
COURSE SERVINGS

1½ lb. salmon filet

½ tsp. olive oil

3 tsp. or less fresh grated
ginger

2 tsp. grated lime zest

2 T lime juice, strained

salt and freshly ground
white pepper

Preheat oven to 500° F. Rinse and dry salmon, remove skin and as many bones as possible. Cut salmon on the bias into ⅛" thin strips or flatten. Brush an ovenproof casserole with olive oil. Arrange salmon scallops on casserole, distribute ginger and lime zest evenly and drizzle with lime juice. Bake salmon until opaque, 3-4 minutes. Don't overcook. Season with salt and pepper. Serve with the following light ginger sauce if desired.

1 T soy sauce
or Passover steak sauce

1 T minced ginger

1 T minced shallots

1 T lime juice

1 tsp. brown sugar

2 T water

Light Ginger Sauce

Simmer all ingredients for 2 or 3 minutes, strain over cooked fish.

SNAPPER FILLETS with CAPER MAYONNAISE - Pareve

SERVES 8 AS AN APPETIZER,
4 AS A MAIN COURSE.

1 lb. boneless fish fillets,
filet of sole or red snapper

1 T olive oil

salt and freshly ground
pepper to taste

4 T lite mayonnaise

1 T prepared white horseradish

4 T drained capers **or** chopped
green olives

lemon wedges

Preheat broiler to high.

Brush broiler pan with oil, place fish on broiler pan in a single layer. Brush fillets with olive oil and season with salt and pepper. Blend the mayonnaise and horseradish. Mash a few of the capers or chopped green olives and mix all of them with the mayonnaise. Brush half the mayonnaise mixture on the fillets and broil close to heat for about 5 minutes. Cool fish, cut into strips. Coat with remaining mayonnaise and garnish with capers or green olives and lemon wedges.

POULTRY

LEMONY CHICKEN BREASTS

SERVES 8

8 to 10   boneless, skinless chicken
       breast halves (2½ lb.)

       juice of one lemon

3   garlic cloves, minced

½   cup olive oil

2   egg whites, lightly beaten

6   T matzo cake meal,
     seasoned with salt, pepper
     and ¼ tsp. ginger

2   scallions, sliced

1   cup mushrooms, sliced

   juice and grated zest of
   1 lemon

1   T sugar

1   cup rich chicken stock

1   tsp. potato starch,
   mixed with 3 T rich
   chicken stock

3   scallions, thinly sliced

¼   cup pimiento stuffed green
   olives

Pound heavy ends of breasts between sheets of wax paper to
cook evenly. Drizzle lemon juice and strew half the garlic
pieces over breasts and turn to marinate for 20 minutes.

Dip chicken in egg whites and lightly coat in matzo cake
meal mixture. Heat 2 T oil in an 11" sauté pan on medium
high. Sauté breasts quickly, 4 minutes per side. Sauté in
batches adding oil as needed. Place chicken breasts in a
shallow, ovenproof casserole. Set aside. May be prepared in
advance up to this point.

Preheat oven to 350° F. Thoroughly heat chicken breasts in
the oven for 15 to 20 minutes.

Strew the hot chicken breasts with scallions, green olives
and sauce. Garnish with additional lemon slices if desired.
Serve immediately.

Lemony Sauce

To prepare sauce, sprinkle mushrooms with a bit of lemon
juice. Combine sugar, remaining lemon juice, broth and
potato starch with lemon zest in a medium saucepan. Bring
to a simmer, stirring constantly, for 3 minutes. Add mushrooms, cook 3 minutes, adjust flavor and consistency with
a bit more chicken stock if needed. Coat chicken breasts
thoroughly, and strew the chicken breast with scallions,
olives.

Preheat oven. Heat chicken 15-20 minutes.

OVEN-FRIED CHICKEN

SERVES 8 TO 10

- 2 fryers, cut up, about 3 to 3 1/2 lb. each

  salt, pepper and garlic salt to taste

- 1/2 cup matzo cake meal **plus** 1 T potato starch

- 2 T paprika

- 1 cup matzo meal

- 2 T parsley leaves, minced

- 1/2 cup orange juice

- 2 egg whites, beaten

- 4 T vegetable oil **or** vegetable cooking spray

Preheat oven to 350° F. Set out a 10 x 2 x 15" baking pan.

Trim chicken of excess skin and fat. Rinse, pat dry. Season to taste with salt, pepper and garlic salt. Mix matzo cake meal and potato starch with 1 T paprika. Dust chicken pieces and place on wax paper. Combine matzo meal, salt and pepper to taste with 1 T paprika in processor for 30 seconds to refine matzo meal. Spread on a baking sheet and toast about 3 or 4 minutes. Cool. Add parsley leaves. Increase oven temperature to 400° F.

Beat egg whites into orange juice in a pie plate. Dip chicken pieces in egg white mixture, allow excess to drip off, then press into matzo meal mixture. Heat pan in oven with 1/2" of vegetable oil or generously spray baking pan. Arrange chicken in a single layer. Bake 20 minutes, turn and bake 15 minutes more. Remove smaller pieces. Turn and bake larger pieces another 10 minutes. Serve hot.

BRAISED CHICKEN THIGHS and DRUMSTICKS

SERVES 8 TO 10

- 6 chicken thighs (about 3 lb.) **and** 8 drumsticks (about 2 lb.)

  salt and freshly ground black pepper

- 2 T olive oil

- 3 T matzo cake meal, **mixed** with 3/4 tsp. paprika

- 1 medium white onion, chopped

- 1 clove garlic, minced

- 3 carrots, peeled, cut in thick slices

- 3 stalks celery, sliced

- 1 cup dry red Passover wine

- 3 cups rich chicken stock

- 2 T tomato paste

- 3 bay leaves

- 1 tsp. lemon thyme, more to garnish

Trim fat and excess skin. If desired, bone the thighs. Season to taste with salt, pepper and dust with matzo cake meal. In a large deep skillet, heat the olive oil on medium high. Arrange the chicken pieces, skin side down in a single layer. Sauté in batches, about 5 minutes per side until golden. Remove chicken pieces to a platter, set aside. Drain all but 1 T of the fat.

Reduce heat to medium, cook onion 5 minutes. Add garlic, cook one minute. Add carrots, celery, wine, stock, tomato paste, bay leaves and bring to a simmer. Return chicken to skillet, add lemon thyme and cover. Cook chicken, turning occasionally, until chicken is just tender, about 25 minutes. With a slotted spoon, lift chicken and vegetables to an ovenproof casserole, discard bay leaves.

Increase heat to high and reduce the cooking liquid to about 2 cups. Pour over the chicken. Can be made ahead to this point and chilled to mature flavor.

Preheat oven to 325° F. Reheat chicken about 30 minutes. Garnish with fresh thyme sprigs and serve from the casserole with a potato kugel.

OLD FASHIONED CHICKEN PAPRIKASH

I always make this especially for our Aunt Annie.

❖ ❖ ❖

SERVES 10

1   T vegetable oil

1   cup onion, chopped

2   cloves garlic, cracked

1/2   lb. necks and giblets

3 1/2   to 4 lb. fryer, cut in 12 pieces

2   T matzo cake meal
    salt and pepper to taste

3   bay leaves

1   tsp. paprika

2   cups chicken stock

In an 8 qt. heavy pot, heat oil and sauté chopped onions until golden. Add garlic, giblets and necks. Sauté 15 minutes, turning occasionally.

Trim chicken pieces of excess fat and some of the skin. Season 2 T matzo cake meal with salt and pepper to taste and 1 tsp. paprika. Dust on chicken pieces. Lightly brown chicken with the giblets, turning frequently until golden. Add bay leaves, chicken stock and cover. Bring to a simmer for 45 minutes. May be chilled overnight at this point. Skim fat.

1   lb. ground beef **or** veal

1   egg white

1   small grated onion

1/2   cup matzo meal
    salt and pepper to taste

1   tsp. dried thyme

3   T matzo cake meal
    mixed with 1/2 tsp. paprika

    vegetable spray

1   can Passover tomato mushroom sauce

The Meatballs

To prepare meatballs, mix together ground meat, egg white, matzo meal, grated onion, salt and pepper and thyme. Form meat into walnut sized balls.

Preheat oven to 425° F. Spray a baking pan with vegetable spray.

On a sheet of wax paper, combine matzo cake meal and 1/2 tsp. paprika. Lightly roll the meatballs in cake meal mixture and place on the baking sheet. Spray meatballs with vegetable spray. Bake 10 minutes, turn meatballs, bake another 10 minutes.

Heat paprikash, add tomato mushroom sauce and meatballs. Gently simmer 30 minutes.

PERSIAN CHICKEN with DATES and ALMONDS

SERVES 8

- 8 boneless chicken breast halves, about 2 1/2 lb.
- juice of one lime
- 1/2 tsp. cinnamon
- 1/2 tsp. ground cloves
- 1/2 tsp. cardamom
- salt and freshly ground pepper to taste
- 2 T matzo cake meal
- 2 T vegetable oil
- 1 generous cup onions, chopped
- 4 garlic cloves, minced
- 1 cup orange juice
- 2 T golden raisins
- 4 T chopped dates
- 4 T toasted sliced almonds

Trim breasts and pound heavy ends to cook evenly. Sprinkle with lime juice, season with cinnamon, cloves, cardamom, salt and pepper, allow to stand 15 minutes. Heat vegetable oil or spray in a heavy 11" non-stick skillet, over medium high heat. Dust chicken with matzo cake meal. Sauté breasts about 4 minutes per side until golden. Remove and keep warm.

Sauté onions and garlic in same pan until limp, 5 minutes. Drain excess oil. Add orange juice, dates and raisins. Simmer 5 minutes, to thicken juices and soften fruit. Return chicken to pan and coat well. Can be made ahead to this point.

Preheat oven to 300° F. Spread almonds in a single layer on a piece of foil, bake 10 minutes. Cover chicken and heat thoroughly, turning to coat several times. Place chicken on serving platter with a slotted spoon, surround with fruit. Increase heat to high and reduce pan juices until thick and syrupy. Pour over chicken, garnish with toasted almonds.

Note: A WHOLE CUT-UP CHICKEN MAY BE USED.

CHICKEN BREASTS in ORANGE SAUCE with PISTACHIOS

SERVES 8

- 8 skinless, boneless chicken breast halves
- salt and pepper to taste
- 4 T matzo cake meal
- 2 T vegetable oil **or** cooking spray
- 1 1/2 cup fresh orange juice
- 1/2 cup minced shallots
- 1/4 cup white wine vinegar
- 1/4 cup white wine
- 2 T brown sugar
- 2 T unsalted pareve margarine, cut up
- 3 T honey
- orange slices and pistachio nuts to garnish

Trim breasts and pound heavy ends under wax paper to cook evenly. Combine salt, pepper and matzo cake meal, dust on breasts.

In a saucepan, bring orange juice, shallots, wine, vinegar and brown sugar to a boil. Simmer and reduce to about 1 cup, keep warm.

Heat vegetable oil or spray in a large skillet over medium heat, sauté breasts in batches 4 minutes per side until springy to the touch. Transfer to an ovenproof casserole, set aside.

Remove sauce from heat and whisk in cold margarine in small pieces. Pour over chicken and keep chicken warm in a low oven. Chicken may be chilled or frozen at this point.

To serve, thoroughly re-heat in a 325° F oven, basting well with the sauce.

Heat honey with 2 T of the orange sauce. Coat orange slices to garnish chicken. Sprinkle with unsalted pistachio nuts.

ROAST CAPON with FRUITED MATZO STUFFING

SERVES 8

1   capon, about 6 to 7 lb.

3   garlic cloves, peeled

1   T unsalted Passover margarine

    salt and fresh ground pepper, paprika

2   sprigs parsley

1   cup white wine

2   cups rich chicken stock, divided

Preheat oven to 375° F. Trim fat.

Rub inside and out with cut piece of garlic and a bit of margarine, season cavity with salt and pepper. Loosely stuff cavity and press 2 sprigs rosemary over the stuffing. Close with a wooden skewer and truss the capon. Bake extra stuffing in a greased casserole with sprig of rosemary and cover with foil.

Set capon on a rack in the roasting pan, add ½ cup stock and roast 30 minutes, reduce heat to 325°F. Baste with pan juices occasionally. Roast a total of about 2½ hours. Cover with foil if skin browns too much. Capon is done when the thickest part of the thigh is pierced and the juices run clear or a thermometer reads 165°. Rest 15 minutes before carving. Simmer 1 cup of remaining rich chicken stock until glossy, add 2 rosemary sprigs, simmer 5 minutes. Pass with the stuffing.

3   cups matzo farfel

2   T vegetable oil

1   onion, chopped

2   medium garlic cloves, lightly smashed

6   dried apricots, chopped

1/4 cup golden raisins

1/2 cup dried currants

1   tart apple, grated

1   egg **and** 1 egg white, lightly beaten

2   T Passover margarine, melted

    several dashes of nutmeg

6   sprigs rosemary

Stuffing

To prepare the stuffing, soak farfel in warm water for 10 minutes. Drain and place in a large mixing bowl. Heat oil, sauté onion until softened, add 1 garlic clove, sauté one minute. Stir into farfel mixture. Plump apricots, raisins and currants in hot water for 10 minutes, drain, pat dry and add to the farfel with the apple. Mix in the egg and egg white and melted margarine. Season to taste with salt and pepper. Allow stuffing to stand for a while to blend flavors and absorb the liquid. Add enough rich chicken stock to keep a loose, but cohesive mixture. May be refrigerated overnight. DO NOT STUFF until immediately before roasting.

TURKEY with SAVORY WILD MUSHROOM STUFFING

SERVES 12 OR MORE

- 4 cups matzo farfel
- 2 T olive oil
- 1 cup onion, chopped
- 3 garlic cloves, minced
- 1 cup celery, chopped
- 2 cups wild mushrooms assorted or other, reserve some for garnish
- 2 shallots, chopped
- salt, pepper and a dash of sugar
- 2 eggs, **plus** one egg white
- 1 cup chicken stock
- 2 T melted Passover margarine
- fennel root or sage leaves, optional

Prepare turkey the same as the stuffed capon. Be sure to defrost poultry 24 hours in the refrigerator to insure maximum moisture and texture.

Savory Stuffing for a 14-16 lb. turkey

To prepare stuffing, soak farfel in warm water for 10 minutes. Drain and place in large mixing bowl. Sauté onions in olive oil until softened, add garlic, sauté one minute, add the celery and mushrooms. Sauté until mushrooms give up their juices. Increase heat to evaporate juices, add shallots. When soft, add to farfel.

Mix in the eggs, egg white, melted margarine and season to taste with salt and pepper. Blanch the fennel root in boiling water three minutes, chop and add with a few fennel sprigs or minced sage leaves. Add enough stock for a moist mixture. Garnish with remaining leaves.

DO NOT STUFF until ready to roast turkey. Calculate about 15 minutes per pound for a stuffed turkey. Bake extra stuffing in a greased casserole.

STUFFED TURKEY ROLLS

SERVES 8

- 8 slices turkey breast 1/2 " thick
- juice of half a lemon
- 2 small zucchini
- 1 carrot, grated
- 1 egg white, lightly beaten
- 1/2 cup parsley, chopped
- 1 tsp. fresh sage leaves or 1/2 tsp. dried
- salt and freshly ground pepper to taste
- 2 T pareve Passover margarine
- 1 medium onion, finely chopped
- 1 clove garlic, minced
- 1/4 cup matzo meal
- 2 T vegetable oil **or** spray
- 1/4 cup matzo cake meal mixed with 1/4 tsp. paprika
- 1 1/2 cups defatted chicken stock

Between sheets of wax paper, pound turkey slices very thin. Sprinkle with lemon juice, set aside.

Grate zucchini, lightly salt and place in a colander to drain 15 minutes. Squeeze out moisture and pat dry, place in a bowl. Add grated carrot, egg white, parsley, sage leaves and season with salt and pepper to taste.

In an 11" non-stick sauté pan, heat margarine, sauté onion until limp, add garlic, sauté 2 minutes. Scrape with the margarine into zucchini mixture. Stir in enough matzo meal to make a cohesive mixture. Taste and adjust flavor.

Divide vegetable mixture onto the 8 turkey slices. Spread in a thin layer, roll up and secure with a toothpick. Dust turkey rolls in matzo cake meal and paprika.

Clean the non-stick sauté pan. Heat oil, quickly brown rolls on all sides. Add stock, cover and simmer until tender, about 30 to 35 minutes. Baste occasionally. If cooking ahead, only simmer 20 minutes and chill turkey rolls separately.

Bring to room temperature to continue. Reduce stock by half, strain over turkey rolls. Heat thoroughly. Garnish with thyme sprigs.

CHICKEN ROULADE with SCALLION SAUCE

SERVES 12

- 4 whole boneless, skinless chicken breasts, about 2½ to 3 lb.
- 12 bay leaves
- juice of one lemon
- 2 T olive oil
- 1 cup white onion, finely chopped
- 3 large garlic cloves, minced
- 3 sweet peppers, one each red, orange and yellow, diced
- 4 to 6 T matzo meal
- 2 T Passover margarine
- 5 cups chicken stock
- 1 tsp. fresh lemon thyme **or** ½ tsp. dried
- salt and freshly ground white pepper
- fresh thyme sprigs to garnish

This recipe only sounds complex. It has many steps, but can be made ahead, and chilled or frozen. It is a beautiful presentation.

Trim chicken breasts. Between two sheets of wax paper, pound each breast to ¼" including thick ends. Be careful not to tear the chicken. On a large piece of parchment paper, center 12 bay leaves. Arrange breasts in a single layer, overlapping each other by one inch to form a continuous rectangle of chicken. Lightly pound edges together. Sprinkle with lemon juice and season with pepper.

Preheat oven to 350° F.

Heat oil in a large sauté pan, cook onions until translucent, 5 minutes. Add garlic, sauté one minute, add the peppers and cook 3 minutes. Remove pan from heat. In same pan, stir in 4 T matzo meal, 4 T chicken stock and 2 T margarine. Season to taste with salt, pepper and thyme. Taste, mixture should be flavorful. Adjust matzo meal to make a loose but cohesive mixture. Spread filling on chicken, to within 2-inches of the edges. Roll 4-inches of the long end of the chicken over the filling once, fold in the short ends. Use the parchment to help finish rolling the chicken.

Tent the parchment and lift the roulade onto a sheet of heavy-duty foil. Pour ½ cup chicken stock inside the parchment, fold over the long sides of the parchment and twist the ends closed. Enclose the roll in foil.

Lift the foil package to a large roasting pan, pour the remaining stock in the pan. Bake 1¼ hours.

Scallion Sauce

2	T olive oil
6	bunches scallions, 5 bunches sliced
2	medium leeks, sliced, whites only
2/3	cup parsley leaves
1	cup chicken stock
1	scant tsp. potato starch
	salt and pepper to taste
1/2	cup green olives, sliced

Heat the oil in a large sauté pan on medium heat. Slowly cook the sliced scallions and leeks until very soft, about 20 minutes. Add the parsley leaves and remove from heat, cool slightly. Puree the mixture until very smooth. Season with salt and pepper. In a medium saucepan, dissolve potato starch in ¼ cup cool chicken stock, cook on low heat, add the scallion mixture and remaining stock. Can be made ahead and re-warmed.

Trim remaining scallions. Make narrow cuts 2 inches from the ends of each scallion and keep the scallion brushes in cold water for garnish.

Cool the chicken roulade 5 minutes. Unroll the foil, drain accumulated liquid and with the parchment paper, slide the roulade onto a platter, seam side down. If scallion sauce is very thick add a few spoons of the pan juices. Spread ½ cup scallion sauce across the roulade. Slice 1" thick. Surround with olives, scallion brushes and thyme sprigs. Pass remaining scallion sauce.

POACHED CHICKEN in WHITE WINE

A very low-fat, flavorful preparation. This will not taste like "soup chicken" if it is well flavored and not overcooked!

EACH FRYER SERVES 4

2	whole fryers, about 3½ lb. each
2	qt. chicken stock
2	T white wine vinegar
1	cup white wine
2	onions, stuck with 2 cloves
10	unpeeled garlic cloves
4	bay leaves
	salt and 10 peppercorns
4	carrots, chopped
4	stalks celery, with leaves, chopped
1	parsnip sliced, optional
10	parsley sprigs
4	sprigs fresh rosemary

Bring fryer to room temperature. Rub inside and out with one cut clove of garlic.

Prepare a stockpot large enough to hold at least one whole fryer, submerged. Trim chicken of excess fat. If cooking one fryer at a time, prepare half the vegetables. Place vegetables and bay leaves in the pot with the stock, white wine vinegar and white wine. Bring to a simmer. Add the chicken and enough water to cover. Cover pot and keep at a simmer, skim occasionally. After 30 minutes, add rosemary sprigs. Keep at a simmer for a total of one hour and 15 minutes.

Lift chicken to platter, rest and carve. Use the same stockpot with remaining vegetables for the second fryer.

Chicken will be very aromatic, but pale. Serve with **Gingered Tomato Avocado Relish** (▶see page 53).

Option: CREATE YOUR OWN SAUCE BY REDUCING 3 CUPS OF THE POACHING LIQUID IN HALF. ADD MORE ROSEMARY OR ½ CUP PASSOVER TOMATO MUSHROOM SAUCE TO COAT CHICKEN. SERVE WITH ONION SLAW.

CORNISH GAME HENS in PLUM SAUCE

SERVES 8 TO 10

4	Cornish game hens
1/4	cup Passover margarine, melted
1/2	tsp. freshly ground white pepper
1	T grated lemon zest
2	oranges, sliced
1/2	cup chicken broth
1/2	cup onions, minced
1	T fresh ginger-root, grated
1/4	cup soy sauce, if available **or** Passover steak sauce
1/3	cup Passover ketchup
6 oz.	frozen lemonade concentrate **or** lemon juice **plus** 2 T sugar
2	16 oz. cans Passover plums with juice (see note)
1/4	cup grated coconut, optional

Preheat oven to 375° F. Halve the hens and trim well.

Brush with 1 T margarine, season with white pepper and grated lemon zest. Arrange orange slices in bottom of a roasting pan to hold hens in a single layer and place them skin side up. Add chicken broth and roast 35 minutes.

Meanwhile, combine remaining margarine, onions, ginger-root, ketchup, soy or steak sauce and lemonade concentrate (or sweetened lemon juice) in a 2 qt. saucepan on medium heat. Puree one can of pitted plums with juice, stir into pan and simmer about 15 minutes. Pour sauce over hens. Roast 25 minutes more, basting frequently. Cool. May be chilled overnight.

Preheat oven to 325° F to reheat. Bring hens and sauce to room temperature.

Reserve juice from remaining can of plums, add to sauce as needed, add plums to pan. Cover with foil and heat thoroughly, basting occasionally. Lift hens to serving platter, cut into quarters. Surround hens with plums and scatter coconut on top. Pass extra sauce.

Note: USE CANNED FRUITS LABELED FOR PASSOVER (OTHERS CONTAIN CORN SYRUP, NOT KOSHER FOR PASSOVER. ALTERNATELY, SIMMER FRESH PLUMS OR TWO PACKAGES FROZEN CHERRIES IN A LIGHT SUGAR SYRUP AND ADD 1 TSP. POTATO STARCH).

GOLDEN ROASTED TURKEY BREAST

SERVES 10 OR MORE

	one whole turkey breast, about 6 to 7 lb.
2	cloves garlic, peeled and slivered
	salt and freshly ground white pepper to taste
1	tsp. ground ginger
1	T pareve margarine
1	tart apple, quartered and cored
1	onion, peeled
2	bay leaves
1	cup rich chicken stock
1/4	tsp. tumeric
1	slice fresh ginger

Trim fatty neck skin and remove large clumps of fat. Place slivers of garlic under the skin, season to taste with salt and pepper. Set apple, onion and bay leaves in cavity. Mix ginger and margarine together, smear half of it on the skin with fingers.

Preheat oven to 375° F. Place turkey in a roasting pan and add chicken stock. Roast 30 minutes, reduce oven temperature to 350° F. Add turmeric to the remaining ginger and margarine mixture. Baste with pan juices and spread margarine on the turkey. Roast 1½ hours or more, basting occasionally, until a thermometer reads 165° F. Rest 15 minutes before carving. Discard bay leaves and onion. The color is beautiful.

Skim and strain pan juices. Simmer with a slice of fresh ginger until slightly reduced, about 20 minutes. Mash ginger slice with pulp of apple and stir into strained pan juices.

Keep warm. Serve turkey warm or at room temperature, pass gravy separately. Serves 10 or more.

Option: GRILL TURKEY BREAST OVER INDIRECT CHARCOAL HEAT ON AN OUTDOOR GRILL TO EASE OVEN SPACE.

TURKEY STUFFED CABBAGE ROLLS

SERVES 12

- 1   head Savoy cabbage
- 1¼ lb. ground turkey breast
- 1   egg
- 1   cup cooked brown rice* **or** 1½ cup baked potato, cooled and grated
- ¾   cup skimmed turkey **or** chicken stock
- 2   T matzo meal
- 1   tsp. fresh **or** 1 tsp. dried sage leaves crushed
- 2   tsp. fresh parsley, chopped
-     salt and black pepper to taste
- 2   T sugar
- 1   tsp. lemon juice
- 1   5-oz. can tomato sauce

Remove core of cabbage; place the head, core down in a large pot with 2" of boiling water or in a steamer set over boiling water. Cover and steam 8 to 10 minutes until softened. Remove at least twelve large leaves of cabbage, shave off thick part of rib. Combine ground turkey, rice or potato, matzo meal, egg, 3 T stock, sage and parsley. Season with salt and pepper to taste.

Preheat oven to 375° F.

Divide the turkey mixture among twelve cabbage leaves. Roll the stem end over the filling, fold in sides and roll up securely. Shred remaining cabbage and scatter in a 10 x 15 x 3" baking dish. Place rolls on top, pour remaining stock over and bake 30 minutes. Baste frequently. Remove 1 cup of the stock and stir in tomato sauce, lemon juice, sugar and a bit more salt. Taste and adjust flavor. Stir the sauce into the pan.

Reduce oven to 325° F and cover with foil. Cook one hour, basting occasionally, until cabbage is very tender. Refrigerate overnight and remove any congealed fat and to improve flavor. Bring to room temperature and re-heat in a 325° F oven one hour.

Note: THE OPTION OF A GRATED POTATO OR RICE IS FOR THOSE WHOSE BACKGROUND PERMITS USING RICE DURING PASSOVER.

TURKEY SCHNITZEL with CRANBERRY SAUCE

SERVES 8

8 turkey cutlets 3/4" thick, about 2 1/2 to 3 lb.

juice of 1/2 a lemon

1 tsp. grated lemon rind

1/4 cup matzo cake meal

1/4 tsp. garlic powder

salt and pepper to taste

1 1/4 cup ground soup mandlen (if available)
or 1 cup matzo meal, finely ground

1 tsp. paprika

2 egg whites

vegetable oil **or** spray for frying

1/4 cup fresh parsley, finely minced

cranberry sauce

Pound each turkey cutlet between sheets of wax paper or plastic until 1/8" thick. Squeeze the juice of half a lemon over the turkey slices. Allow to marinate 10 minutes.

Season matzo cake meal with pepper, garlic powder and lemon rind, place on a piece of waxed paper. Mix paprika into ground soup mandlen or matzo meal on another sheet of waxed paper. Lightly beat egg whites with a dash of salt and 2 T water in a shallow pie plate.

Cut large turkey slices in half and dust with matzo cake meal mixture, shake off excess. Dip into egg whites, drain excess, dredge in mandlen or matzo meal and place on a baking sheet. Chill 15 minutes.

Coat a non-stick pan with vegetable oil or spray and heat to medium high. Sauté turkey slices 2 minutes per side until golden. Place on baking sheet. May be made in advance to this point. Chill or freeze in single layers separated by parchment paper.

Bring to room temperature and reheat in a 325° F oven for 15 minutes. Sprinkle with parsley or serve with cranberry sauce.

Note: MAKE THIN SLICED VEAL THE SAME WAY.

NUTRITIONAL ANALYSIS (excluding sauce)

Total Calories: 314	Carbohydrate:18g (23%)	Protein: 42g (53%)
Fat: 8g (24%)	Cholesterol: 97g	

2 cups cranberry juice

3 T frozen cranberry juice concentrate

1/4 cup orange juice

1 T orange zest

1 tsp. lemon juice

1 tsp. potato starch

2 T light brown sugar

1/4 cup dried cranberries

orange slices, optional

Cranberry Sauce

Simmer first 4 ingredients in a medium saucepan until reduced nearly in half to intensify flavor. Dissolve potato starch in 1 T cold water, slowly stir into pan. Add cranberries, lemon juice and simmer until they plump. Taste and adjust sweetness with brown sugar. Add thinly sliced oranges to garnish. Pass with the schnitzel.

CRUSTED TURKEY LOAF

SERVES 8

5	slices of matzo
2	T vegetable oil **plus** vegetable spray
1/2	lb. Passover turkey kielbasa or wieners
1	cup chopped onions
3	chopped garlic cloves
1/2	lb. dark meat turkey, cut in 1" cubes
1	tsp. fresh chopped sage **or** 1/2 tsp. dried
21/2	lb. ground turkey breast **or** combined light and dark meat
1	whole egg **and** 2 egg whites
2	cups baked potatoes, cooled, peeled and grated
1/2	cup matzo meal, divided
2 to 3	T prepared Passover steak sauce
	salt and pepper to taste
1	tsp. fresh **or** 1/2 tsp. dried thyme leaves
3/4	cup turkey or chicken stock

Peel outer skin from the sausage and mash or dice the pieces. Heat a large nonstick skillet, spray lightly and add sausage pieces. Slowly sauté, about 6 minutes. Remove to a medium bowl. Sauté the onions in the same pan until translucent, add oil as needed. Add the garlic and cubed turkey breast, sauté about 5 minutes until meat is no longer pink. Combine with the cooked sausage, 3 T matzo meal, 2 T egg white and sage leaves. Add enough steak sauce to color the mixture.

Combine the ground turkey, egg, remaining egg whites, matzo meal, grated potatoes, salt, pepper and thyme leaves. Loaf should be moist, and very flavorful. Add a bit of stock as needed. Sauté a spoonful to taste if desired.

Spray a 2 lb. loaf pan with vegetable oil. Moisten 3 slices of Matzo in warm water, quickly drain and line the bottom and sides of the pan with 3 slices of matzo. Spray with oil.

Preheat oven to 350° F.

Spread a thick layer with half the ground turkey mixture over the matzo. Slightly indent the center and arrange the chopped turkey-sausage mixture, cover with remaining ground turkey. Press loaf together firmly. Pour ½ cup stock over the loaf. Dip remaining matzo in warm water, cover loaf. Spray with vegetable spray and cover loaf with foil. Bake 1¼ hours. Uncover and spray top matzo with vegetable spray, bake 15 minutes to brown. Cool 10 minutes before slicing. Can be made ahead and re-heated. Garnish with fresh thyme sprigs.

Serve with cranberry sauce or **Candied Sweet and Sour Beets**. (▶see page 51).

Note: SHAPE LOAF IN GREASED FOIL AND PLACE IN A LARGER PAN, IF A LARGE LOAF PAN IS UNAVAILABLE.

BEEF

ROAST EYE of the RIB

SERVES 10 OR MORE

6 to 8	lb. eye of the rib, well trimmed, single piece
3	cloves garlic, slivered
1	tsp. kosher salt, freshly ground pepper
1	cup dry red Passover wine
1	cup beef stock
1	medium onion, sliced
8	oz. sliced mushroom

Not low cholesterol! This wonderful main course requires little preparation time and is very easy on the cook! Serve moderate portions and offer lots of vegetable options.

Trim excess fat; cut narrow slits at random in roast, insert garlic slivers, season with pepper to taste. Set roast on a rack in roasting pan and pour ¼ cup of wine on roast.

Preheat oven to 475° F.

Pour ¼ cup stock and remaining wine over roast. Center in the oven and roast 30 minutes; reduce heat to 350° F. Continue cooking 8 minutes per pound for rare, 10 minutes per pound for medium. If fat drips and tends to splatter, add ¼ cup water to the pan. Do not open door during the first hour of roasting time.

Reduce remaining stock to ½ cup. Oil or spray an 11" sauté pan with olive oil, sauté the onion 5 minutes, add mushrooms. Sauté until limp, about 5 minutes, add reduced stock and season to taste with salt and pepper. Set aside.

When roast is at desired doneness, remove to a cutting board for 15 minutes. Carve and trim excess fat. Arrange on serving platter. Add a few spoons of the au jus to the mushroom sauce and pass separately.

Our local kosher butcher claims he can barely keep enough briskets in the shop at Passover!

ROAST BRISKET OF BEEF WITH BARBECUE SAUCE

SERVES 10 TO 12

6 to 7 lb. beef brisket, first cut

    powdered garlic, salt and pepper, to taste

1 cup Passover barbecue sauce

1 package Passover onion soup mix

1 cup Passover ketchup

1 cup brown sugar

1 cup vinegar

From Nina Wain, who claims her family fights for every crumb of this brisket

Preheat oven to 375° F.

Trim brisket of excess fat. Season to taste with garlic, salt and pepper.

Heat sauce ingredients together for 3 minutes and pour over brisket in roasting pan. Cover and roast 30 minutes. Reduce temperature to 325° F, baste brisket and cook another 1½ to 2 hours, until brisket is tender, basting frequently. (Brisket may be chilled at this point and reheated.)

Remove excess fat, slice against the grain. Arrange beef on platter and strain sauce over sliced beef. Keep warm.

JUST GOOD BRISKET - PLAIN and SIMPLE

SERVES 10 TO 12

5 to 6 lb. beef brisket

3 cloves garlic, slivered

    salt, pepper, ½ tsp. paprika

½ T vegetable oil **or** pareve margarine

2 onions, sliced

2 carrots, chunked

2 bay leaves

2 celery stalks

4 sprigs parsley

1 cup beef stock **or** water

½ cup red wine, optional

Bring meat to room temperature. Trim brisket of visible fat. Preheat broiler to medium high.

Cut several slits in brisket at random, insert half the garlic slivers. Combine salt and pepper to taste with paprika and make a paste with the oil or margarine. Spread on top of the brisket. Place brisket on a rack about 5 inches from broiler, sear until top is crusty.

Preheat oven to 375° F.

Set brisket in a large roasting pan. Surround with remaining vegetables, 2 bay leaves, and stock or water. Cover and roast 30 minutes. Reduce oven temperature to 325° F. Roast 2 hours or until meat is fork tender. (May be chilled at this point. Strain gravy and vegetables, chill separately.)

Remove brisket to platter. Trim fat from brisket and slice before reheating. Discard fat from gravy, add ½ cup red wine and simmer to reduce and intensify flavor. Reheat brisket and vegetables at 325° F moistened with ½ cup of the reduced gravy. Serve with Potato Zucchini Kugel and pass extra gravy.

FESTIVE SWEET BRISKET with FRUIT

5 to 6 lb. brisket of beef, preferably
        first cut

1 large white onion, sliced

2 cloves garlic, slivered

1 cup sweet red wine

1 cup non-fat beef stock

2 bay leaves

6 peppercorns

8 to 10 pitted prunes

8 to 10 dried apricots

1/2 cup golden raisins

24 Belgian carrots

2 T brown sugar **or** honey

Trim brisket of all visible fat. Cut slits at random into meat and insert some garlic slivers. Place onions and remaining garlic in a large roasting pan, add red wine. Place brisket in pan, turn to coat with wine several times for 30 minutes.

Preheat oven to 375° F.

Add beef stock, bay leaves and peppercorns to pan. Cover and roast 30 minutes. Reduce temperature to 325° F, roast one hour, basting occasionally. Add prunes, apricots, carrots and raisins. Coat with pan juices, add more wine and beef stock as needed. Roast 1½ hours more or until meat is fork tender. If brisket needs a longer cooking time, remove vegetables and fruits when they are tender.

It's best to remove brisket slightly undercooked, chill it, trim fat and slice one day ahead. Discard bay leaves.

Return sliced brisket to skimmed pan juices to absorb maximum flavor overnight.

Add brown sugar or honey to pan juices. Reheat at 325°F. Baste sliced meat well. Serve surrounded with fruits and carrots and potatoes.

Options: USE DRIED CRANBERRIES, DRIED CHERRIES OR OTHER FRUITS.

TRADITIONAL EUROPEAN BEEF TSIMMES

SERVES 8

6 to 8 beef bones
       or 3 lb. flanken

3 to 4 lb. boneless chuck roast
       or 2nd cut brisket

   4   lb. white baking potatoes,
       peeled, cut in 2" chunks

   2   lb. sweet potatoes, peeled,
       cut in 3" chunks

   1   lb. carrots, peeled, cut in
       1" slices

   1   medium onion, chopped

   1   cup pitted prunes

 1/2   cup each dried apricots
       and raisins, optional

 1/2   cup each granulated
       and dark brown sugar

11/2   tsp. kosher salt, 1/2 tsp.
       pepper to taste

   1   tsp. sour salt, or more

   2   T potato starch

   2   T honey

This is a one-pot meal. Since I always offer a chicken dish as well, I serve the potato-carrot mixture separately. The thick sweet and sour potato gravy is delicious.

❖ ❖ ❖

Preheat oven to 350° F.

Rinse and trim fat from bones and meat. Place bones or flanken on bottom of a 12 qt. heavy roasting pan. Scatter prepared potatoes, carrots and onion on top, add 1 tsp. salt and pepper. Fill pan with water to cover vegetables about halfway. Place boneless chuck or second cut brisket on top. Cover pan and roast one hour. Reduce oven to 325° F. Tilt pan occasionally to keep vegetables moist, roast one hour more. Add remaining salt, sour salt and sugars; taste and adjust flavor. Add prunes and optional fruits. When chuck or brisket begins to soften, remove to a platter, cover and chill separately. Tsimmes is best if flavors mature overnight.

Next day, skim congealed fat from vegetables and juices, slowly heat Tsimmes in a 325° F oven. Adjust the sweet and sour flavor with more or less sour salt and sugar. Often a little more salt brings the flavors together.

Trim fat and cut meat into thick slices. Remove one cup of warm pan juices to dissolve potato starch and stir back into pan juices. Heat thoroughly with the sliced meat, moistened with pan juices. Serve separately or combine in deep bowls. Drizzle with honey. Tsimmes improves with age.

*A **potato kugel** (▶see page 37) on top of the tsimmes is the piece-de-resistance. My grandmother's specialty was to make a big potato kugel, more like a dumpling, cooked in the heavy liquid across the top of the entire tsimmes. Remove the cover the last 20 minutes to brown.*

BEEF TAGINE with ONIONS, PRUNES and RAISINS

SERVES 6 TO 8

- 2 T red wine vinegar, **or** red wine
- 2 lb. boneless beef chuck, well trimmed, cut into 2" or smaller cubes

  salt and freshly ground pepper to taste

- 2 T matzo cake meal, **mixed** with 1 tsp. paprika
- 2 T olive oil
- 1 lb. onions, (about 3) sliced
- 2 cup beef stock or water
- 1 bunch cilantro, or (parsley) rinsed and tied with a string
- 1/8 tsp. Spanish saffron powder **or** crushed threads
- 2 T ground turmeric
- 2 tsp. ground ginger
- 1 cup pitted prunes
- 2 tsp. ground cinnamon
- 1/2 cup honey
- 1 1/2 cup raisins, soaked in warm water and drained
- 2 T pistachios, unsalted

Sprinkle beef with wine vinegar, salt and pepper to taste and allow to marinate 30 minutes. Dust beef with matzo cake meal mixture. Heat oil in heavy 6 qt. pot or Dutch oven on medium heat. Add onions, lightly salt, cook 5 minutes, add a dash of sugar and cook slowly for 20 minutes to caramelize. Push the onions to the side of the pan or remove. In batches, add meat and brown on all sides. Drain excess fat. Return onions to pan.

Add 2 cups stock or water, cilantro, saffron, turmeric and ginger, stir to combine. Cover and cook on medium low heat, stirring occasionally and add small amounts of water if necessary. Simmer until beef is fork tender, about 1½ to 2 hours. Stir in prunes, cinnamon, and honey.

Add raisins during last 15 minutes of cooking time. Season to taste with salt and pepper. Discard cilantro. Freezes well. Defrost and heat in microwave or moderate oven.

Spoon into a serving bowl and sprinkle with pistachios. Serve with apple matzo kugel.

NUTRITIONAL ANALYSIS

Total Calories: 654
Fat: 26g (36%)
Carbohydrate: 78g (47%)

Carbohydrate: 18mg
Protein: 27g (17%)
Fiber (g)/ Alcohol: (%) 5g (0%)

CORNED BEEF with PINEAPPLE BROWN SUGAR GLAZE

SERVES 10

6 to 8 lb. pickled brisket, first cut preferably

1 T pickling spices, optional

Set the pickled brisket in a wide ovenproof Dutch oven and cover with water. On medium heat, bring to a simmer for 30 minutes. Taste the cooking liquid. If it's bland add pickling spices; if it's very salty, change the water. Cover and simmer another 30 minutes.

Preheat oven to 350° F.

Drain about half the boiling liquid, cover pan and place in the oven. After 30 minutes, taste cooking liquid again. If very salty, remove more cooking liquid and add fresh water. Roast until just tender, about 2 to 2½ hours total. Turn frequently to keep moist.

1 cup dark brown sugar

1 can pineapple chunks, 20 oz.

1 tsp. ground ginger

Glaze

Drain pineapple and reserve the chunks. Boil pineapple juice, brown sugar and ginger together until syrupy, add about ½ cup cooking liquid from the roasting pan.

Uncover meat and discard all but 1-inch of cooking liquid. Generously brush corned beef with the glaze. Continue cooking and basting until corned beef is very tender and well glazed. It is tastiest if served without chilling. However, it can be made ahead and slowly re-warmed. Slice corned beef and arrange on serving platter. Heat remaining glaze and brush over meat. Garnish with the pineapple chunks. Keep warm or serve room temperature.

WIENER GOULASH

SERVES 8

1 T vegetable oil **or** cooking spray

2 onions, chopped

8 large all beef **or** veal wieners, cut in 1 1/2 " chunks

1 clove garlic, optional

2 carrots, sliced

1 can 10 oz. Passover tomato mushroom sauce

3 large baking potatoes, boiled and cubed

An old fashioned favorite my grandmother made at lunch for all the kids. Imagine my surprise when my mother-in-law made it, too.

In a 4 qt. heavy pot, heat oil and sauté onions until lightly browned, about 5 minutes. Add wiener pieces and sauté until wieners give off their juices, drain any fat. Add carrots, cover with 1 cup water and tomato mushroom sauce, cook 15 minutes. Add potatoes, simmer 15 minutes. Serve with Passover rolls and a salad for lunch.

SPAGHETTI and MEATBALLS

1½ lb. ground boneless chuck steak (**or** ground turkey **or** combination)

1 medium onion, grated

salt and freshly ground pepper to taste

1 garlic clove, crushed

3 to 4 T matzo meal

2 egg whites

2 T matzo cake meal

1 tsp. paprika

vegetable **or** olive oil spray

MAKES 8 CHILDREN'S PORTIONS

1 tsp. olive oil

1 onion, diced

3 oz. fresh mushrooms, sliced

2 cans Passover tomato mushroom sauce

1 T fresh oregano, chopped **or** ½ tsp. dried

1 T fresh basil, chopped **or** ½ tsp. dried

fresh minced parsley

Prepare **Passover "noodles"** (▶see page 18). Keep dough rolled and wrapped in plastic. Refrigerate until sauce is prepared.

Meatballs

Mix ground meat with grated onion, garlic, matzo meal and season with salt, pepper and ½ tsp. paprika. Add as many egg whites as necessary to make a cohesive mixture. Form walnut-size meatballs, about 1½ inches in size. Season cake meal with salt, pepper and paprika, lightly dust meatballs in cake meal. Spray a heavy baking sheet with vegetable spray and arrange meatballs, chill 30 minutes.

Preheat oven to 425° F. Spray tops of meatballs, bake 10 to 12 minutes, shake once or twice to brown all sides. Set aside.

The Sauce

Heat olive oil in a 10" sauté pan. Cook onions until golden, add mushrooms and sauté until they exude their juices and the liquid evaporates. Add tomato mushroom sauce, oregano, basil, parsley and simmer 5 minutes. Taste, add more herbs to taste. Heat meatballs in the sauce or keep separately. Can be prepared to this point one day ahead.

To serve, remove noodles from refrigerator. Slice to desired thickness and gently stir into tomato sauce so meatballs don't break the "spaghetti" heat thoroughly.

Adults love these, too.

NUTRITIONAL ANALYSIS

Total Calories: 251
Fat: 8g (28%)
Carbohydrate: 25g (38)
Sodium: 130mg

Cholesterol: 55mg
Protein: 21g (33%)
Alcohol: 0g (0%)
Fiber: 2g

LAMB

MIDDLE EAST LAMB KEBABS

MAKES 8 GENEROUS SERVINGS
2 1/2 lb. lean ground lamb
1/2 cup fresh parsley leaves, minced
4 T coriander leaves, minced
4 T lime juice
2/3 cup onion, grated
1 large egg
3/4 tsp. cinnamon
3/4 tsp. ground cumin
2 to 4 T matzo meal
salt and freshly ground pepper to taste
1/4 cup pine nuts **or** pistachios
mint leaves

In a large bowl, combine the lamb, parsley, coriander, lime juice, grated onion, egg, cinnamon and cumin. Mix well. Add enough matzo meal for a cohesive mixture. Form the mixture into 16 ovals about 3" long and 2" wide. Place on a foil-lined pan, chill several hours.

If desired, thread each lamb oval onto two skewers and grill over a charcoal fire. Alternately sauté in a non-stick pan or broil kebobs on a foil lined broiler pan.

Preheat broiler to medium high and set rack 4" from heat. Broil the lamb kebobs about 4 minutes per side, until cooked through and well browned. Garnish platter with pine nuts or pistachios and mint leaves. Serve with fresh mint chutney.

Note: Make small kebobs for appetizers and lunch, larger ones for main courses.

FRESH MINT CHUTNEY

4 oz. fresh mint leaves
4 T chopped onion
cayenne pepper, optional
1 T chopped fresh ginger
1 1/2 tsp. sugar
salt and pepper to taste
1 T cider vinegar

Combine all ingredients in a food processor. Add 1 T water and adjust to taste with salt, pepper and sugar. Refrigerate in a small jar. Can be made 2 days ahead.

MINA — A GREEK STYLE MEAT PIE

SERVES 8

4 T vegetable **or** olive oil

2 cups chopped onions

1 T minced garlic

1½ cups thinly sliced mushrooms (8 oz.)

2 cups cooked lamb **or** chicken, minced

2 T matzo meal

salt and pepper to taste

1 cup chopped parsley

½ lb. fresh spinach, chopped

1 whole egg and 3 egg whites, lightly beaten

8 slices matzo

1 cup chicken stock

Heat 3 T oil in an 11" skillet, add onions, slowly sauté 5 minutes. Add garlic, cook 2 minutes, until transparent. Add mushrooms. Increase heat when mushrooms exude their juices to evaporate most of the liquid. Cool slightly. Stir in meat, matzo meal, season to taste with salt and pepper. Add ½ cup parsley, the chopped spinach and half the beaten eggs. Remove from heat.

Preheat oven to 350° F. Lightly oil a 9 x 13" baking pan.

Quickly dip matzo into stock to soften, arrange a single layer in pan. Spoon half the meat mixture over matzo, cover with a second matzo layer, spread remaining meat mixture, top with matzo. Brush top matzo with oil, pour over remaining stock and egg mixture, bake 15 minutes. Brush again with oil, continue baking 15 minutes more. Cool 5 minutes before slicing.

NUTRITIONAL ANALYSIS

Total Calories: 251	Sodium: 130mg	Alcohol: 0
Fat: 8g	Cholesterol: 55g	Fiber: 2g
Carbohydrate: 25g	Protein: 21g	

ROASTED LAMB SHANKS

SERVES 8

6 lb. lamb shanks, trimmed extra bones, if available

juice of half a lemon

vegetable spray

1 cup onions, chopped

2 cloves garlic

1 cup carrots, sliced

¼ cup matzo cake meal

salt, pepper and paprika to taste

1¼ cups veal **or** chicken stock

½ cup dry white wine

2 T fresh rosemary leaves, sprigs to garnish

Season lamb shanks with salt, pepper and sprinkle with lemon juice. Keep at room temperature 30 minutes. Coat or spray a large heavy skillet with vegetable oil. Sauté onions 5 minutes until translucent. Add garlic and carrots, cook 5 minutes. Brown extra bones in the same pan. Remove to a large, heavy roasting pan.

Mix matzo cake meal with salt, pepper, paprika and dust on lamb shanks. Add oil as necessary. In batches, brown shanks on all sides in the same skillet and add to the roaster.

Preheat oven to 350° F.

Add veal stock and white wine to skillet. Stir, scraping up all bits and bring to a boil for 5 minutes. Strain over lamb shanks in roaster, add rosemary leaves. Cover and roast about 1¾ hours until tender. May be slightly undercooked and chilled. Skim fat and reheat the next day. Serve hot garnished with fresh rosemary. The weight of lamb shanks can be deceiving, as there is a large bone.

Note: VEAL SHANKS CAN BE USED FOR THIS RECIPE.

VEAL BRISKET with TOMATOES and BALSAMIC VINEGAR

SERVES 8

5 lb. veal brisket

salt, freshly ground pepper and paprika to taste

1 medium onion, chopped

2 carrots, peeled and chopped

2 cloves garlic, minced

1/2 cup dry white wine

1½ to 2 cups skimmed veal **or** chicken stock

3 T balsamic vinegar

1½ cups ripe, chopped plum tomatoes

1 T fresh rosemary leaves, sprigs to garnish

12 grape tomatoes

Preheat broiler to 425° F. Trim veal brisket of excess fat and place in roasting pan. Season brisket with salt, pepper and paprika. Sear meat on both sides close to the broiler, until well browned.

Reduce oven temperature to 325° F.

Scatter brisket with onions, garlic, carrots and add wine, 1 cup of stock and half the tomatoes. Cover and roast 1½ to 2 hours, basting occasionally. Add stock as needed.

When brisket is tender, with a slotted spoon, lift the pan vegetables into a 2 qt. saucepan. Add ⅔ cup of cooking liquid, remaining tomatoes, balsamic vinegar and rosemary. Simmer 15 minutes. Strain over the veal. Puree vegetables and add to the pan juices. (May be made ahead to this point and chilled.)

Skim fat from pan juices before reheating. Rest the veal brisket or chill it. Slice against the grain. Return to the oven with the skimmed gravy and vegetable puree for about 30 minutes or until meat is tender. Garnish with rosemary and grape tomatoes.

VEAL with PEPPERS in TARRAGON SAUCE

Adapted from Andras Olgyai at Gundel Restaurant in Budapest

SERVES 8

4 T pareve margarine, divided

4 T olive oil, divided

1 medium onion finely chopped

1 small red bell pepper, cut into julienne

1 small green bell pepper, cut into julienne

4 T matzo cake meal **mixed** with 1 T potato starch

1 cup or more chicken **or** veal stock

3/4 cup dry white wine

3 T fresh tarragon leaves, and sprigs to garnish

1¾ lb. veal scallops

salt, freshly ground pepper to taste

Melt 2 T margarine in a large, heavy sauté pan on medium heat. Add onion, cook until softened, about 5 minutes. Add peppers and sauté about 10 minutes. Remove vegetables to a bowl. Pour wine into pan, stir and scrape up browned bits. Whisk in 1 T margarine kneaded with 1 T cake meal into potato starch mixture, stir 3 minutes. Season with salt and pepper, whisk in stock, bring to a simmer, stirring until thickened. Add tarragon and adjust seasoning. Keep warm.

Pound meat to ⅛" thick, dredge in remaining cake meal mixture, shake off excess. Heat more margarine and oil in another heavy sauté pan on medium high heat. Sauté veal in batches on both sides until pale gold in color, about 2 minutes per side. Add margarine and oil as needed. Add to the pan of onions and peppers, simmer 10 to 12 minutes, until tender, turn to coat well.

Arrange on a deep platter. Scatter onions and peppers over veal and strain sauce on top. Garnish with tarragon leaves. Serve with potato knishes.

STUFFED BREAST of VEAL - TWO WAYS

MAKES 6 CUPS

- 3 cups matzo farfel
- 4 T vegetable oil
- 2 cups chopped onions
- 1 red **and** 1 yellow pepper, cut into julienne
- 8 T parsley, minced

  salt and freshly ground black pepper, paprika
- 2 tsp. fresh rosemary leaves
- 3 cups chicken or veal stock, divided

Prepare this stuffing recipe for either a boneless breast of veal or a veal breast with bones. The boneless option is easier to serve at a Seder. A veal breast with bones doesn't go very far. Insist that the butcher give you the bones. They make a wonderful stock and an excellent rack on which to cook the boneless stuffed veal breast.

Make the Stuffing

Soak matzo farfel in water 5 minutes, drain. Place in a large mixing bowl. Sauté onions in oil until limp. Add the peppers, parsley, salt and pepper, cook 10 minutes. Add to farfel with rosemary leaves and ½ cup stock or more, enough to bind stuffing mixture. Set aside. Bake extra stuffing during last hour of roasting time in a greased casserole. (May be prepared one day ahead.)

SERVES 10 OR MORE

- 6 to 8 lb. boneless breast of veal **or** 8 to 10 lb. veal breast, cut with a pocket

  juice of one lemon
- ½ cup white wine
- 3 garlic cloves, minced
- 2 large onions, sliced
- 8 cloves garlic or more, unpeeled
- 4 carrots cut in 1" chunks

Prepare the Veal Breast

Trim visible fat from veal, set roast on a large piece of parchment paper. Sprinkle 1 T minced garlic and 2 T white wine on veal breast with bones inside the pocket. Sprinkle both sides of either type veal breast with remaining garlic, onions, white wine and lemon juice. Season to taste with salt and pepper. Allow to marinate chilled for 30 minutes.

Preheat oven to 375° F. Place prepared vegetables in a large roasting pot.

Stir stuffing, keep mixture loose, fill pocket of veal breast on the bones. Close with a wooden skewer. Place over the vegetables in a large roasting pan, pour over remaining chicken stock, cover and roast 30 minutes.

Pound heavier ends of boneless veal breast for easier rolling. Spread stuffing about 1" thick across center of boneless veal and sprinkle with minced garlic. Use parchment paper to help roll. Tuck in the ends. Fasten with cotton string. Make a rack of the bones if you have them, in the roasting pan. Place veal roll on top, strew with vegetables and add stock. Cover with foil and roast 30 minutes.

Reduce oven temperature to 350° F, continue roasting about 2 to 2½ hours, basting occasionally. (May be refrigerated overnight at this point.) Remove foil to crisp meat during the last 15 minutes. When fork tender, place veal on cutting board for 10 minutes.

Strain pan juices, skim fat. Simmer pan juices until reduced by one third or serve with lemon sauce.

Slice veal between ribs into serving portions. Slice boneless breast of veal about 1-inch thick. Serve with pan juices or lemon sauce.

NUTRITIONAL ANALYSIS (excluding lemon sauce)

Total Calories: 589	Sodium: 130 mg	Alcohol: 0
Fat: 16g (25%)	Cholesterol: 55 g	Fiber: 2 g
Carbohydrate: 45g	Protein: 21g	

The Lemon Sauce

2 T potato starch

2 T Passover margarine, melted

   juice of ¹/2 lemon, 1 tsp. grated lemon zest

1 cup veal cooking juices, strained

In a small pot, combine potato starch with a bit of cool stock to dissolve. Place on medium low heat, add lemon juice, margarine and slowly warm. Add cooking juices. Adjust flavor with salt and pepper as desired. Pass the sauce separately.

VEAL and MUSHROOM RAGOUT

SERVES 8

2 to 2¹/4 lb. boneless veal cut in 1" cubes

2 T lime juice

4 T matzo cake meal

   salt and freshly ground pepper to taste

2 T olive oil

1 large white onion, sliced

2 cloves garlic, minced

1 carrot, peeled and sliced

1 T paprika

2 cup rich veal **or** chicken stock

10 oz. shiitaki mushrooms, thickly sliced

¹/2 cup dry white Passover wine

¹/4 cup parsley, minced

Trim meat, sprinkle with lime juice and marinate 15 minutes. Combine 1 tsp. of the paprika, salt and pepper with the matzo cake meal. Dredge the meat in the matzo cake meal mixture.

Heat 2 T olive oil in an 11" sauté pan on medium high heat. Sauté onions 5 minutes, add garlic and sauté 3 minutes. Push onions to the side of the pan. Add veal pieces, quickly brown on all sides. Add carrot, stock and bring to a simmer. Stir in remaining paprika and cover pan. Simmer about 1½ hours, until meat is very tender. Add more stock or water as needed.

Toss mushrooms with white wine, add to pan, simmer 5 minutes more. Spoon veal ragout into a preheated deep serving bowl with all the liquid. Sprinke with parsley. Serve with Passover "noodles" or potato kugel.

Note: THIS CAN BE MADE WITH LEAN BEEF.

SEPHARDIC MEAT PIE

SERVES 12 AS SIDE PORTIONS,
8 AS MAIN COURSE PORTIONS

2 T vegetable oil

1½ cups chopped onions

1 clove garlic, minced

1½ lb. ground lamb
or chicken

½ tsp. turmeric

1 tsp. ground cinnamon

¼ cup feathery dill, minced,
more for garnish

salt and freshly ground
pepper, to taste

3 T matzo meal

2 T tomato paste

2 whole eggs, 2 whites

6 slices of matzo

freshly ground nutmeg

Preheat oven to 375° F. Grease a 9 x 13" ovenproof pan with 1 tsp. oil.

Heat remaining oil in an 11" sauté pan on medium heat (or spray a non-stick pan with vegetable spray). Add onions, sauté until limp, 5 minutes. Add garlic and meat, stir and cook until meat browns. Remove from heat, add 2 T dill, turmeric, cinnamon, salt and pepper to taste. Pour off excess fat, cool. In a small mixing bowl, lightly beat 1 whole egg, add to meat mixture with tomato paste and matzo meal.

Beat remaining whole egg and egg whites with 3 T water and a dash of salt in a pie plate. Hold matzo slices under warm water for a few seconds to soften. Drain and place on wax paper. Dip 2 or 3 matzo slices in the egg mixture, line the pan. Spread meat mixture on matzo, sprinkle with remaining dill. Repeat with remaining matzo to cover the meat. Pour extra egg on matzo and grate nutmeg on top.

Bake 15 minutes; reduce oven to 350° F, bake 40 to 45 minutes until top is golden and crusty. Cover with foil if it browns too much. Uncover last 5 minutes and brush top with water to crisp. Cool 5 minutes before slicing into squares to serve.

Note: MAKE EARLY IN THE DAY, REHEAT IN A 300° F OVEN. MATZO MAY BE A BIT SOGGY IF FROZEN.

VEGETARIAN MAIN COURSES

ROASTED VEGETABLE PYRAMIDS - Dairy

SERVES 8

1/2 cup olive oil

1 lb. eggplant, cut crosswise into 1/3 " slices

1 1/4 lb. zucchini, sliced into 1/3" slices

2 medium red onions, sliced 1/3 " thick

1 lb. medium red potatoes, sliced 1/3 " thick

salt and freshly ground pepper

4 large plum tomatoes, 1 1/4 lb. cut lengthwise into 1/3" slices

1/2 lb. mozzarella cut into 6 slices of 1/4 "

3/4 cup ricotta cheese

1 1/2 tsp. chopped fresh basil or thyme leaves

6 fresh rosemary sprigs, trim bottom leaves

A delightful dairy vegetarian alternative main course.

Preheat oven to 450° F. Brush two baking pans with olive oil.

Arrange vegetables, except tomatoes, on pans in a single layer. Brush with olive oil and season with salt and pepper. Roast vegetables in batches, in middle and lower third of oven 8 minutes. Turn vegetables and switch pans, roast 8 minutes more until crisp tender. Transfer to a baking sheet in single layers, separated by wax paper. Can prepare one day ahead.

Bring to room temperature to proceed. On an oiled baking sheet, alternate layers of eggplant, onion slices, mozzarella, potatoes, zucchini and ricotta cheese. Season each layer with salt, pepper, basil and a few rosemary leaves. Top with tomatoes. Make 8 vegetable pyramids.

Preheat oven to 425° F.

Insert wooden skewer through center from top to bottom. Bake in middle of oven about 15 minutes or until thoroughly hot and cheese melts. Trim rosemary sprigs to 1 inch higher than vegetable stacks, remove skewer and insert rosemary sprig. Serve with a green salad.

SPINACH MOUSSAKA - Pareve or Dairy option

SERVES 6 TO 8

4   matzo slices

1¼ lb. fresh spinach, stems removed
     or 2 pkg. (10 oz.) frozen
     spinach

1   medium onion, and 2
     garlic cloves, chopped

6   T vegetable oil

1   lb. chopped mushrooms

2   T almonds, finely chopped

     salt and freshly ground
     pepper to taste

2   tsp. lemon juice

1   T feather dill leaves, minced

2   T matzo meal

2   eggs **plus** 1 egg white

1½ cups mashed potatoes

     grated nutmeg

Preheat oven to 400° F. Grease a 9" square pan with 1 T oil.

Briefly dip matzo slices in water to soften. Drain on paper towels. Fit 2 matzo slices on bottom of pan. Thoroughly drain frozen spinach. Wash fresh spinach, remove stems. Cook fresh spinach in salted water for 2 minutes, drain and chop.

Sauté onion and garlic in 2 T oil until golden, add the mushrooms. Cook until mushroom juices evaporate. Season with salt and pepper, add the spinach, lemon juice and almonds, remove from heat. Cool. Lightly beat 2 eggs with a pinch of salt, stir into spinach mixture. Adjust flavor and add dill and a bit of matzo meal if needed.

Brush matzo in pan with oil and spread with potatoes. Top with the spinach mixture, cover with remaining matzo and brush with oil. Beat the egg white with 1 T oil, add nutmeg and brush on matzo. Bake 50 minutes, baste with remaining egg white and grated nutmeg several times. Bake until top is lightly browned. Serves 6 as a main course.

Note: ADD 1 CUP RICOTTA CHEESE TO THE SPINACH MIXTURE FOR A HEARTY PASSOVER DAIRY MEAL.

EGGPLANT MOUSSAKA - Vegetarian

2	eggplants, about 1 lb. each, sliced, unpeeled
4	large potatoes, peeled, thinly sliced
1/4	cup olive oil
2	onions, chopped
2	cloves garlic, minced
1 1/2	lb. mushrooms, sliced
1	can (14 oz.), plum tomatoes, seeded and chopped
	pinches of cinnamon, nutmeg, and sugar
1/4	cup parsley, chopped
2	T fresh oregano leaves **or** 1tsp. dried
	salt and pepper to taste
3	eggs, separated (discard one yolk if desired)
1/3	cup matzo meal
	freshly ground nutmeg

A delicious lighter alternative.

Salt eggplant slices and place in colander. Weight with a plate and a heavy can on top, drain 30 minutes. Rinse, pat dry. Boil potatoes 7 minutes, drain, drizzle with 1 T olive oil, set aside.

Meanwhile, heat 2 T olive oil, sauté onions until golden, add garlic, and sliced mushrooms. Sauté until mushrooms give up their juices and are lightly browned. Add tomatoes, cook 3 or 4 minutes. Add spices, sugar, oregano, parsley, salt and pepper to taste.

Preheat oven to 350° F. Oil a deep 9 x 13" pan.

Line pan with potato slices, spread 4 T of tomato mixture over potatoes, add eggplant slices, sprinkle with matzo meal, continue layering, ending with potatoes, using all the sauce.

Beat egg yolks with 1 tsp. olive oil and a dash of salt until creamy. Beat whites until stiff, fold in the yolk mixture. Spread over the Moussaka, sprinkle with nutmeg and bake 45 minutes. Flavor improves if refrigerated overnight. Bake 10 minutes less if preparing in advance.

Bring to room temperature, cover and reheat at 325° F, for 30 minutes. Cool briefly. Cut into small squares to serve as an appetizer or 12 large squares as a main course.

ELEGANT STUFFED PEPPERS - Dairy

SERVES 6

- 3 large red sweet peppers
- 1/2 lb. eggplant
  kosher salt, freshly ground black pepper
- 1 1/2 lb. tender zucchini
- 3 scallions, sliced
- 1/2 yellow pepper **and** 1/2 red pepper, diced
- 1/4 cup olive oil
- 4 T matzo meal
- 1/4 cup red wine vinegar
- 1 garlic clove, chopped
- 1 egg, lightly beaten
- 1/2 lb. Passover Swiss cheese, grated
- 1 T each fresh oregano, parsley and basil, minced whole leaves to garnish
- 1/3 cup grated Passover Parmesan cheese

Roast the peppers over a flame or under broiler until charred on all sides, about 20 minutes. Cool in a brown paper bag. Peel, remove seeds and ribs, cut peppers in half.

Cube the eggplant and sprinkle with salt. Drain in a colander for 30 minutes. Rinse and dry. Slice zucchini in half lengthwise, cut crosswise into thin slices.

Preheat oven to 400° F.

Heat 2 T olive oil in a deep sauté pan on medium heat, add scallions and sauté 5 minutes. Add the eggplant cubes, sauté 5 minutes. Add more oil as needed to sauté the zucchini and diced peppers, cover and cook 15 minutes. Spoon the vegetables into a bowl and stir in red wine vinegar, garlic and matzo meal. Gently mix in the egg, grated cheese and season to taste with salt, pepper and herbs.

Oil a baking pan to hold the peppers in a single layer. Brush the pepper halves with olive oil and divide the prepared mixture into the peppers. Bake 20 minutes. Sprinkle peppers with grated Parmesan cheese, bake 5 minutes more. Garnish with fresh basil leaves or parsley sprigs. Serve hot. A delicious main course.

Note: PREPARE STUFFED ZUCCHINI OR YELLOW SQUASH IN THE SAME MANNER. HALVE SQUASH LENGTHWISE, SCOOP OUT SHELLS TO 1/2". SALT AND DRAIN, THEN PROCEED AS ABOVE. USE INSIDE OF SQUASH FOR FILLING.

Passover Pavlova with Strawberry sauce

Brownie Pie

DESSERTS

"He swore unto thy fathers to give thee a land flowing with milk

and honey..." —**Exodus 12:24**

"And the house of Israel called it Manna and it was like coriander seed,

white; and the taste of it was like wafers made with honey...."

—**Exodus 16:31**

Medley of Sorbet

LET THEM EAT CAKE!

Passover baking depends on beaten egg whites to replace other leavening agents. Flourless Passover cakes rise or fall with the egg whites. In classes, my students were pleased to learn that properly beaten, egg whites can raise Passover baking to new heights—you can too.

Egg whites contain only 17 calories, albumen, protein and water. Correctly beaten, tiny air bubbles trapped in the protein portion increase the volume six or seven times, for light and fluffy cakes. If beaten too much or too little, the results are disastrous.

Underbeaten, egg whites are watery and dull; overbeaten, they are dry. Egg whites need to be stabilized with either a copper bowl or an acid. (Cream of tartar is not kosher for Passover.) Adding salt first delays foaming; after beating it won't incorporate. Cold and fat deter egg whites from mounting. It's a delicate balance.

Hints for Success

- Finish other recipe phases before beating the whites.

- Place cold eggs in warm—not hot—water for 15 minutes to warm, then proceed.

- Eggs separate best when cold, beat best at room temperature.

- Carefully separate eggs; a speck from the yolk prevents mounting.

- Use an absolutely clean, round-bottomed metal bowl, preferably copper, to stabilize egg whites. Whites slip in glass bowls, plastic usually absorbs fats and aluminum discolors whites as does copper, *if* cream of tartar is added.

- Rinse bowl in hot water with a few drops of lemon juice, rinse again and dry. This simulates a copper bowl.

- Use a balloon whisk or electric mixer with whisk attachment at medium high speed.

- Once started, *do not stop beating*—whites won't mount if interrupted.

- To every 4 egg whites at room temperature, add ⅛ tsp. salt after 60 seconds, when whites are foamy and starting to softly peak. Add ½ tsp. water to stiffen egg whites for meringues after 60 seconds.

- Gradually increase to medium high speed; constantly move hand beater or whisk around bowl.

- Beat until all whites are softly peaked and lightly curl as beaters are lifted.

- Slowly add spoons of sugar. Beat until stiffly peaked; whites stand straight up if beaters are lifted. Stop before whites are dry.

- Use whites immediately after fully beaten. Fold, do not stir into base mixture.

To Fold, spoon ¼ of whites on base mixture. With a large rubber spatula, cut through center of batter, turn scraper and pull it through batter along bottom. Lift batter with egg whites up the side of bowl and flip over to center. Rotate bowl one-quarter turn, repeat. Work with quick, smooth strokes; incorporate nearly all whites into base mixture. Fold in whites in three additions. It should take two to three minutes or egg whites will deflate.

Do practice. The technique is worthwhile —especially at Passover.

CAKES

THE BASIC SPONGE CAKE - Pareve

SERVES 16

10 eggs, room temperature, separated

1½ cups sugar

¼ tsp. salt

juice of one lemon, strained

juice of one orange, strained

1 T each, finely grated orange and lemon zests

¾ cup matzo cake meal

¾ cup potato starch

1 cup walnuts, finely chopped, optional

My mother-in-law made her sponge cake in this unusual manner. Most recipes beat whites and yolks separately then fold, yet this works perfectly.

Preheat oven to 325° F. Set out a clean two piece 10" ungreased tube pan.

In the large bowl of an electric mixer on medium speed, beat egg whites until foamy, add salt, increase speed to medium high. Slowly add sugar, beat until whites are stiff and glossy. Reduce speed, add yolks one at a time. Add juices and zests alternately with sifted dry ingredients. Fold in nuts by hand. Don't over-beat.

Spoon batter into pan. Bake about 1 hour and 10 minutes or until center of cake springs back when lightly touched. Cool 5 minutes, invert pan to cool completely. Run a knife around sides of pan to remove outer pan. Run a knife under bottom and center post of pan. Set cake on plate, store airtight.

Note: I OMIT 3 EGG YOLKS AND REPLACE EACH YOLK WITH ONE EGG WHITE, 1 TSP. WATER OR JUICE TO RETAIN TEXTURE. ADDING ONLY EXTRA EGG WHITES CREATES A TEXTURE AKIN TO AN ANGEL FOOD CAKE.

Variations: Replace ½ cup of the dry ingredients with ½ cup sifted cocoa powder. Fold in ½ cup grated semi-sweet chocolate or ¾ cup miniature chocolate morsels.

THE VERSATILE JELLY ROLL - Pareve

4   eggs, room temperature,
    separated

3/4 cup extra fine sugar, divided

2   tsp. lemon juice

1   tsp. grated lemon zest

5   T potato starch

    pinch of salt

    Passover confectioner's sugar

Preheat oven to 350° F. Grease a 10 by 15" jellyroll pan. Line with parchment paper, allow ends to overhang 1".

In a large bowl of an electric mixer, beat one whole egg and 3 yolks until thick and color lightens. Gradually add all but 2T sugar, the lemon juice and zest. Sift potato starch over mixture and incorporate with a rubber scraper.

In another large clean bowl, with clean beaters, beat 3 egg whites until foamy on medium low speed. Add a pinch of salt, gradually increase speed, add 2 T sugar, beat until shiny and stiff.

Fold whites into yolk mixture in three additions. Spread the batter evenly in prepared pan. Bake 25 minutes. Cake will spring back when lightly touched. Spread a towel on the counter and lightly sift with Passover confectioner's sugar. Turn cake onto towel, remove paper, gently roll up cake in towel and cool. May be chilled to fill later.

Fill with purchased Passover pudding or apricot filling. Dust with Passover confectioner's sugar. Garnish with chocolate dipped apricots. Cut into 12 slices,

APRICOT FILLING - Pareve

12   oz. dried apricots, diced

1 3/4 cup water

3   strips orange zest

2   T fresh lemon juice

1/2 cup sugar

2   T Passover orange liqueur
    or white wine

1   T Passover confectioner's
    sugar

6   large whole apricots
    for garnish

1   oz. semi-sweet chocolate

A tasty filling for a layer cake or jelly roll to keep cholesterol down!

In a medium pan, combine diced apricots, water, lemon juice and orange zest. Bring to a simmer, cover. Cook 20 minutes until water is reduced to half and apricots are soft. Stir in sugar, cook on low uncovered to thicken mixture and evaporate liquid.

Remove from heat, cool 10 minutes. Transfer to processor. Puree until smooth, add 2 T orange liqueur or wine; consistency will be like mayonnaise. Transfer to bowl, cover and chill one hour or more. Bring to room temperature. Thin if necessary or filling may break the delicate jellyroll or layer cake. Assemble cake, sift with 1 T confectioner's sugar.

Melt chocolate, coat half of each whole apricot in chocolate. Chill on wax paper to set chocolate. Garnish the apricot filled cake.

STRAWBERRY FILLING - Pareve

1 package whole frozen strawberries

1/2 cup sugar

1 T orange juice

1 tsp. lemon juice

1½ T potato starch

1 pt. fresh strawberries, sliced

Defrost strawberries. In a 2 qt. pan, heat berries, juices and stir in sugar to dissolve. Combine potato starch with 3 T of strawberry juice.

On low heat, add potato starch mixture and cook stirring constantly until thick and translucent. Cool. Add half the sliced strawberries. Fill a jellyroll or cake and chill. Trim with fresh strawberries.

FROZEN LEMON MOUSSE - Dairy

SERVES 12

6 slices of sponge cake

2 T white wine

4 egg yolks

1/2 cup **plus** 2 T sugar

6 T fresh lemon juice

4 T unsalted butter
or Passover margarine

1½ T grated lemon zest

2 pkg. plain Passover gelatin

dash of salt

1½ cups heavy cream, whipped

Line a 10" springform pan with plastic. Arrange cake slices over bottom and partially up sides of pan. Sprinkle with white wine.

Blend egg yolks and ½ cup sugar in a non-corrosive pan. Add lemon juice, butter or margarine and salt. On low heat, cook until thick and light in color, stirring constantly. Mixture will thicken and coat the back of a wooden spoon. Do not boil. Strain into a bowl and add the zest. Cool.

Dissolve gelatin in 2 T cold cream. Warm until liquid is clear.

In a cold bowl of an electric mixer, beat cream until thickened, add gelatin. Increase speed; gradually add 2 T sugar and beat until stiff. Fold cream into lemon mixture. Pour into prepared pan, cover with plastic and freeze overnight.

Remove sides of pan. Slice frozen as mousse defrosts quickly despite the Passover gelatin.

APRICOT MOUSSE - Pareve - low fat

SERVES 8

6 oz. dried apricots, chopped

1½ cups water

½ cup super fine granulated sugar **or** honey

3 tsp. lemon juice

3 T Passover apricot liqueur or brandy

4 large egg whites, room temperature

pinch of salt

Combine apricots and water. Simmer until apricots soften, about 15 minutes.

Cool slightly and process apricots to a puree with 3 T of cooking liquid, sugar or honey, lemon juice and liqueur or brandy. Spoon into large bowl.

With electric mixer, beat egg whites on low speed until foamy, add salt. Increase speed to medium high and beat until stiff but not dry. Fold whites into warm apricot puree in three additions. Spoon into bowl or fill cake and chill. Garnish with **chocolate dipped** or **glazed apricots** (▶see page 125).

ALMOND TORTE - Pareve

SERVES 12

½ cup sliced almonds, toasted

6 to 8 almond-flavored macaroons

4 oz semi-sweet chocolate, cut up

1 T water

1 cup pareve Passover margarine

1 cup sugar

5 eggs, separated

½ cup sifted matzo cake meal

Passover confectioner's sugar

mint leaves for garnish

Preheat oven to 350° F. Grease a 9" springform pan, line with parchment paper, grease paper and dust with cake meal. Toast almonds on a piece of foil in oven for 5 minutes, set aside.

Process macaroons, measure ⅓ cup crumbs and reserve. Melt chocolate and 1 T water in top of double boiler, cool.

Beat margarine and all but 2 T sugar in bowl of electric mixer until creamy, add yolks one at a time, beat until light and fluffy. Gradually add matzo cake meal alternately with macaroon crumbs and fold in chocolate.

In a clean bowl with clean beaters, beat egg whites, add a dash of salt. Increase speed, add 2 T sugar and beat until stiff but not dry. Fold into batter in three additions.

Pour batter into prepared pan. Bake 40 to 45 minutes until a toothpick inserted in center comes out clean. Cool in pan on a wire rack 15 minutes, remove outer pan, cool completely. Invert onto serving dish and remove parchment. Sift with Passover confectioner's sugar. Garnish with toasted almonds and mint leaves.

Note: AN ADDITIONAL ⅓ CUP GROUND ALMONDS AND ½ TSP. PASSOVER ALMOND FLAVOR CAN REPLACE MACAROONS.

CHOCOLATE ELEGANCE - Pareve

10 large eggs, separated, room temperature

1¼ cup sugar

½ cup matzo cake meal

½ cup potato starch

½ tsp. instant coffee powder

1 tsp. unsweetened cocoa

½ tsp. vanilla
or 1 T vanilla sugar

¼ cup orange juice

pinch of salt

few drops of lemon juice

1¼ cups finely chopped walnuts

5 oz semi-sweet chocolate, grated

chocolate mousse
(▶see following page)

Make one day ahead. Cover with plastic, fill three hours before serving.

Preheat oven to 350° F. Set rack in lower third of oven. Set out a perfectly clean two-piece 10" tube pan, ungreased.

In the large bowl of an electric mixer, beat yolks and 1 cup sugar until thick and pale yellow. Sift together cake meal, potato starch, coffee and cocoa. Add alternately with vanilla and orange juice.

Rinse another large bowl and beaters in cold water and a few drops of lemon juice, dry. Add egg whites, beat at medium low speed 60 seconds, add a pinch of salt, increase to medium high speed. Slowly add remaining sugar, beat until stiff, but not dry.

With a large rubber scraper, fold one-fourth the beaten egg whites into the yolk mixture to lighten; quickly fold in remaining whites in two additions. Fold in nuts and grated chocolate.

Scrape batter into prepared pan. Center cake pan on rack, reduce oven to 325° F. Bake 60 to 70 minutes. Cake is done when it springs back when lightly pressed in center.

Cool in pan 5 minutes. Invert to cool completely for one hour. Run a thin spatula around sides to remove outer pan. Slide spatula under bottom and post, set cake on serving dish. Cool completely. Chill or freeze, covered with plastic. Prepare mousse and chill.

To Assemble, stir mousse 2 or 3 minutes until color deepens. Slice cold cake in half crosswise, fill with one-third of the mousse. Replace top, frost top and sides with remaining mousse. Refrigerate at least two hours. Cover cake with a rigid dome when cold. To serve, grate remaining chocolate on cake.

Option: PASS MOUSSE SEPARATELY.

CHOCOLATE MOUSSE - Pareve

SERVES 8 TO 10

6   large eggs, room temperature
     pinch of salt
1¼   cups sugar
8   oz. semi or bittersweet
     chocolate, chopped
¼   cup red wine
1¾   sticks pareve margarine,
     room temperature
1   tsp. vanilla **or** vanilla sugar

To be safe, this recipe "cooks" the eggs in a double boiler. Not as fluffy, this method works well for fillings.

Place eggs in a large metal bowl of electric mixer. Set bowl over a pan half full of simmering water. With a whisk or hand mixer on low, beat eggs, add a pinch of salt, slowly add sugar. Beat about 3 minutes. Increase speed, beat until eggs are thick and lemon-colored, 3 or 4 minutes more. Eggs will feel very warm. Don't let them "cook." Place bowl on stand of electric mixer, beat on medium 5 minutes to cool completely.

Melt chocolate in another bowl over hot water. When soft, stir in the wine. Remove from heat, add margarine one tablespoon at a time. When smooth, slowly beat into the egg mixture until smooth. Chill. Stir down air bubbles to fill cake or pie.

COLD CHOCOLATE MOUSSE - Pareve

SERVES 8 TO 10

6   oz. semi-sweet chocolate
     plus 1 oz. for garnish
6   T sugar
¼   cup water
5   large eggs, separated
¼   tsp. instant coffee powder
¼   tsp. Passover vanilla
     or 1 tsp. vanilla sugar
     pinch of salt
     finely grated rind of
     one orange

Melt 6 oz. chocolate, 5 T sugar and water in top of double boiler set over hot, not boiling, water. Stir occasionally until smooth, remove from heat. Meanwhile, in a large mixer bowl, beat yolks until thick and pale yellow. Stirring constantly, incorporate very warm chocolate mixture with yolks. Add coffee and vanilla.

In a clean bowl with clean beaters, beat whites on medium speed and add a pinch of salt. Increase speed to medium-high. Slowly add 1 T sugar, beat until stiff, not dry. Add rind.

Fold whites into chocolate mixture in three additions. Do not over-mix. Chill in serving bowl or individual cups. Garnish with grated chocolate. Delicious by itself.

Note: I USED THIS RECIPE FOR YEARS WITH NO PROBLEM—EXCEPT THERE'S NEVER ENOUGH!

ANGEL FOOD CAKE - Pareve - No Fat
or Cholesterol

SERVES 12 OR MORE

- 3/4 cup potato starch
- 1/4 cup matzo cake meal
- 1 T vanilla sugar
- 1½ cups egg whites, room temperature
- 1¾ cups sugar
- 1/4 tsp. salt
- 1 T lemon juice
- 1 T almond liqueur **or** orange juice
- 1/2 tsp. Passover almond extract, optional

Preheat oven to 325° F. Set out a perfectly clean two-piece 10" tube pan.

Combine matzo cake meal, potato starch and ½ cup sugar, sift three times, set aside.

In a large bowl of an electric mixer, beat egg whites on low speed until foamy, add salt and increase speed to medium high. Beat until softly peaked. Gradually add remaining sugar and vanilla sugar, one tablespoon at a time. Beat until stiff and glossy, about 10 minutes. Add lemon juice, almond liqueur or orange juice and almond extract. With rubber spatula, quickly fold in the matzo cake meal mixture. Do not over-mix.

Gently pour into pan, smooth top. Bake 50 to 60 minutes until top is golden and springs back when lightly touched in center.

Remove from oven, rest 3 or 4 minutes, invert cake pan an inch above counter. If pan doesn't have metal feet, suspend on inverted spoons or cans. Cool completely. Loosen sides of cake with a thin spatula, remove outer pan. Slide spatula under cake and around post to remove bottom of pan. Wrap airtight with several layers of plastic. Do not freeze.

Serve with strawberry sauce, fresh strawberries or meringue frosting.

MERINGUE FROSTING - Pareve

- 3 egg whites **plus** a pinch of salt
- 2 T water
- 1 T fresh lemon juice **or** lime juice
- 2/3 cup vanilla sugar
- 1 tsp. honey
- 3 T strawberry jam, optional

In a metal bowl of electric mixer, beat egg whites, water, lemon or lime juice and vanilla sugar one minute. Set bowl over a pot of hot, not boiling, water. Beat 7 to 8 minutes with hand-held mixer on medium-high speed. Meringue will be very warm and stiffly peaked.

Place bowl on mixer stand, beat until cool, about 5 minutes. Add honey or optional jam. Frosting is like marshmallows. Quickly spread on cake. Meringue can be baked until golden in a 350° F oven for 5 minutes. Prepare two hours ahead.

CHOCOLATE TRUFFLE CAKE - Dairy

by Kathy Fleegler, past Director Culinary Institute, University Hospitals Synergy, Cleveland, OH

SERVES 8 TO 10

- 2 oz. semi-sweet chocolate, finely chopped
- 1/2 cup unsweetened Dutch Process cocoa powder
- 2/3 cup **plus** 1/4 cup sugar
- 2 T potato starch
- 1/2 cup skim milk
- 1/4 cup coffee
- 1 large egg, **plus** 1 egg white
- 1 tsp. Passover vanilla
- 2 large egg whites
- 7 or 8 small dried apricots, soaked 20 minutes in 3/4 cup boiling water

  boiling water

Preheat oven to 350° F. Lightly spray sides of an 8 x 2" round cake pan with vegetable spray. Line bottom of pan with parchment paper.

Place chopped chocolate in large bowl. In a medium saucepan, combine cocoa with 2/3 cup sugar and potato starch. Gradually whisk in enough milk to form a smooth paste, then add remaining milk and coffee. Bring to a simmer over moderate heat, stirring constantly with a wooden spoon. Simmer gently 1 or 2 minutes. Pour hot cocoa mixture over chocolate. After 30 seconds, whisk until smooth. In small bowl, lightly beat whole egg and egg white with vanilla. Add to chocolate.

In blender or food processor, puree apricots with enough soaking liquid for about 1/4 cup of smooth puree.

With an electric mixer, in a clean bowl with clean whisk beater, beat 2 egg whites at medium speed until softly peaked. Gradually add 1/4 cup sugar, increase speed to medium high and beat until whites are stiff, not dry.

Add pureed apricots to chocolate mixture. With a large rubber spatula, fold 1/4 of the beaten egg whites into the chocolate mixture. Fold in remaining whites. Scrape batter into prepared pan and smooth top. Set the cake pan in a larger baking pan in the lower third of the oven. Pour enough boiling water to reach halfway up sides of cake pan. Bake 30 minutes, until cake springs back when gently pressed in center. The cake will still be quite wet inside, but firms as it cools. Remove cake from water bath, cool on a rack. Cover with plastic wrap, refrigerate overnight or up to 2 days.

To serve, invert pan on a plate covered with wax paper. Peel off paper on bottom of cake, invert cake onto serving plate.

Option: SERVE WITH A SAUCE OF PUREED FROZEN RASPBERRIES, SWEETENED TO TASTE OR APRICOT SAUCE.

NUTRITIONAL ANALYSIS:

| Total Calories: 118 | Fat: 2g | Carbo: 25g | Sodium: 26g |
| Cholesterol: 18mg | Protein: 9g | Fiber 1g | Alcohol: 0% |

CHOCOLATE APRICOT TORTE - Pareve

SERVES 8 TO 10

- 1/4 cup finely chopped dried apricots
- 1/4 cup Passover brandy
- 1/8 tsp. Passover almond extract
- 6 oz. semi-sweet chocolate
- 1/2 cup pareve margarine
- 3 large eggs, separated
- 3/4 cup granulated sugar
- 2/3 cup blanched almonds, ground
- 1/4 cup matzo cake meal
- 1 T potato starch
- 1/4 tsp. salt
  - Glazed Apricots **or** Chocolate Glaze, to garnish

Preheat oven to 350° F. Grease an 8" springform pan, line with parchment paper, grease again.

Soak apricots in brandy and almond extract one hour. In top of double boiler over hot water or in microwave on medium power, melt chocolate and margarine. Stir until smooth. Cool slightly.

In large bowl of electric mixer, beat yolks and ½ cup sugar until light and thick, about 5 minutes. Stir in chocolate mixture, almonds, matzo cake meal, potato starch and apricots with soaking liquid.

In another large clean bowl of electric mixer with clean beaters, beat egg whites until foamy, add salt. Increase speed to medium high and beat until softly peaked. Slowly add remaining sugar one tablespoon at a time. Fold whites into yolk mixture in three additions. Pour batter into prepared pan. Bake until a toothpick inserted in center comes out clean, about 35 minutes.

Cool in pan 15 minutes. Loosen cake with a spatula, remove outer pan and cool completely. Invert onto serving dish. Remove bottom of pan and parchment. Wrap in plastic and store chilled up to 3 days. Garnish with **chocolate glaze** (▶see below) and glazed apricots.

GLAZED APRICOTS - Pareve

- 3/4 cup sugar
- 3/4 cup honey
- 1/2 cup water
- 16 or more whole soft, dried apricots

In a one-quart saucepan, combine sugar, honey and water. On medium heat, stir until sugar dissolves and add apricots. Cook, stirring frequently until apricots are tender and cooking liquid is very thick, about 20 minutes. Cool several hours in syrup. Drain apricots on wax paper to set glaze. Keep 3 days chilled

CHOCOLATE GLAZE - Pareve

- 6 oz. semisweet chocolate
- 1/4 cup sugar
- 1/4 cup water
- 1/4 cup pareve margarine, room temperature

In top of double boiler over hot water or in microwave on medium power, melt chocolate with sugar and water. Remove from heat and stir in margarine. Cool until thickened. Spread on cake.

BANANA NUT CAKE - Pareve

SERVES 12 TO 14

vegetable oil
or vegetable spray

7   eggs, separated (to lower fat
    and cholesterol, use 5 yolks
    and 9 whites)

1   cup sugar

    juice of half a lemon
    and 1 T grated lemon zest

3   very ripe bananas, mashed
    (1¼ cups)

½   tsp. salt

¼   cup potato starch

¾   cup matzo cake meal

1   cup finely chopped walnuts

Preheat oven to 350° F. Lightly grease or spray a 9 by13"
pan with vegetable oil, dust with matzo cake meal.

In large bowl of electric mixer, beat yolks on medium
speed, gradually add ½ cup sugar and lemon juice, beat
until pale and thick, about 5 minutes. Stir in bananas, salt,
lemon zest and sift in potato starch and cake meal. Blend
well, add nuts.

In another large clean bowl with clean beaters, beat whites
at medium speed one minute, add a dash of salt. Increase
speed to medium high, gradually add remaining sugar and
beat until whites are stiff but not dry. Fold whites into yolk
mixture in three additions.

Pour batter into prepared pan, bake about 40 minutes
until a wooden skewer inserted in center comes out clean.
Cool completely in pan on a rack. Frost with honey glaze
or sift with Passover confectioner's sugar. Cut in squares.
(Half a recipe makes 12 delicious muffins.)

HONEY GLAZE - Pareve

⅓   cup honey

⅓   cup brown sugar, packed

¼   cup Passover margarine,
    melted

1   T water

Combine all ingredients in small pan on medium heat, stir
until well dissolved. Cool to lukewarm, pour over cooled
cake to glaze.

MOCHA COFFEE GLAZE - Pareve

2   T hot water

1   T instant coffee powder

¼   cup firmly packed dark
    brown sugar

1   tsp. potato starch

1   T finely grated chocolate

In a small heavy saucepan, dissolve coffee powder in water.
On medium heat, add sugar and potato starch, stir constantly. Simmer until thick, remove from heat. Stir to relax
bubbles, add chocolate. When smooth, pour on cooled
cake. Allow to set until firm.

"CHAROSET" APPLE CAKE - Pareve

SERVES 10

8   firm apples, peeled, cored and diced

5   T Passover margarine

3/4   cup sugar, divided

3   large egg yolks, 4 egg whites

    pinch of salt

3/4   cup golden raisins

1   cup matzo meal

1/4   cup sugar

1/2   tsp. ground cinnamon

3   T sliced almonds

3/4   cup Passover confectioner's sugar

3   tsp. lemon juice

Preheat oven to 350° F. Grease a 9" springform pan and dust with cake meal.

On medium heat, melt 2 T margarine in a heavy 11" sauté pan. Cook apples, stirring often as they exude their juices. Evaporate most juices, don't scorch. Spoon into a large bowl, coarsely mash apples. Add remaining margarine and ½ cup sugar or to taste. Cool briefly. Stir in egg yolks and raisins.

With mixer on low speed, beat egg whites until foamy, add salt, increase speed and beat until stiff but not dry. Fold whites into the apple mixture in two additions.

Combine matzo meal, ¼ cup sugar and cinnamon. Sprinkle half cup of mixture into prepared pan. Spoon half the apple mixture into prepared pan, spread with all but 4T matzo meal mixture. Spread remaining apples, top with matzo meal mixture and sliced almonds. Bake until golden and firm to the touch, about 45 to 50 minutes. Cool.

Combine confectioner's sugar, lemon juice to taste and 1 tsp. water. Drizzle on cooled cake.

LOW-FAT PINEAPPLE CAKE - Pareve

SERVES 10 TO 12

1/3   cup potato starch

1/4   cup matzo cake meal

1/2   tsp. each ground ginger and ground nutmeg

1/4   tsp. salt

10   egg whites, 5 egg yolks at room temperature

2/3   cup extra fine sugar

3   T frozen pineapple juice concentrate, defrosted

1½   tsp. each finely grated orange and lemon zest

1/2   cup blanched almonds, ground

1   T Passover confectioner's sugar

Preheat oven to 325° F. Line a perfectly clean 9 or 10" tube pan with parchment paper.

Sift together first four ingredients, set aside. Wipe large bowl of electric mixer with the cut side of a lemon to remove any traces of grease, wipe dry. Place egg whites and salt in cleaned bowl. Place yolks in another large bowl.

With whisk attachment, beat whites until foamy, slowly add ½ cup sugar, beat until stiff and glossy. In second bowl, beat yolks until light and thick, add remaining sugar, zests and pineapple juice.

Fold half the whites into the yolk mixture. Fold yolk mixture back into whites with 12 quick strokes to incorporate the batters. Sift dry ingredients over egg mixture; in 12 quick strokes, incorporate. Fold in nuts, spoon into prepared pan. Bake 55 minutes.

Cool 5 minutes. Turn upside down to cool cake completely. Run a thin spatula or knife around cake pan and set on serving platter. Dust with confectioner's sugar. Serve with peppery grilled or canned pineapple. Do not freeze.

FLOURLESS CHOCOLATE NUT CAKE - Pareve

Adapted from Executive Chef James Cohen

SERVES 8 TO 10

- 1 cup pecans
- 1 cup hazelnuts
- 1 cup almonds
- 1 cup walnuts
- 7 oz. high quality bittersweet, not unsweetened, chocolate, chopped
- 3/4 cup sugar
- 8 large eggs, separated, room temperature
- 1 tsp. freshly grated lemon zest
- 1 T freshly grated orange zest
- 1 T cocoa powder

Preheat oven to 350° F. Lightly grease a 9" springform pan and line with parchment paper. Set rack in lower third of oven.

In batches, process nuts until finely ground. Finely grind chocolate with 6 T sugar.

In the bowl of an electric mixer, beat egg yolks until thick and pale, add chocolate mixture, the zests and combine well.

In a large clean bowl with clean beaters, beat egg whites until foamy, add a pinch of salt and slowly add remaining sugar. Beat to soft peaks. Gently but quickly, fold the nut mixture alternately with the egg whites into the yolk mixture. Fold until just combined.

Scrape batter into prepared pan and center on oven rack. Bake 55 minutes, until a tester comes out clean. Cool on a rack and remove pan. Can be made one day in advance. Dust with cocoa powder.

Note: A VERY RICH CAKE; I ELIMINATED TWO EGG YOLKS AND USED 10 WHITES WITHOUT SERIOUS RESULTS DUE TO THE LARGE AMOUNT OF NUTS.

CHOCOLATE NUT PASSOVER CAKE - Pareve

SERVES 12

- 9 eggs, separated, room temperature
- 1 1/2 cups sugar
- 2 T fresh orange juice
- 1 T fresh lemon juice
- 1 T freshly grated orange zest
- 1/3 cup potato starch
- 1/3 cup matzo cake meal
- 1/3 cup unsweetened cocoa
- 1/2 tsp. salt
- 1/2 cup finely ground walnuts **or** pecans
- 1 T cocoa powder

Preheat oven to 325° F. Set out a perfectly clean ungreased two piece 10" tube pan.

In large bowl of an electric mixer, beat yolks until thick and pale, gradually add 1 cup sugar. Beat until mixture is thick and pale. Add orange and lemon juices and orange zest. Sift dry ingredients together. Gradually add to yolk mixture, beat just until combined.

In another clean bowl, with clean beaters, beat the whites at medium low speed until frothy, add salt, beat until softly peaked. Increase speed to medium high, add remaining sugar a spoonful at a time. Beat until whites are stiff but not dry. Fold whites into chocolate mixture in three additions. Gently fold in walnuts.

Pour batter into pan and bake for 55 to 60 minutes until a cake tester comes out clean. Invert pan above counter to cool thoroughly. Run a thin sharp knife around edges of post and pan to remove. Sift with cocoa powder.

TURKISH NUT CAKE - Pareve

From Hevra Goodman, fellow cooking teacher at Synergy

24 SQUARES

- 5 eggs, room temperature
  pinch of salt
- 1 cup sugar
- 1/4 cup vegetable oil
  juice and grated zest of one orange
- 2 tsp. ground cinnamon
- 1¼ cups fine matzo cake meal
- 1¼ cups blanched almonds, finely chopped

Cake

Preheat oven to 350° F. Lightly oil a 9 x 13" pan.

Beat eggs until frothy, add salt and beat 30 seconds more. Slowly add sugar, beat continuously until thick and light in color.

Add remaining ingredients, one at a time, beating until each is well incorporated. Pour batter into prepared pan, bake 30 to 35 minutes. Cool on a rack 2 or 3 minutes to relax steam.

Slowly pour half of cooled syrup over warm cake. Add more as syrup is absorbed. Cool at least two hours. Cut in small squares, as it's very sweet.

- 2 cups sugar
- 2 cups water
- 2 tsp. lemon juice

Syrup

Stir sugar and water together, in a 2 qt. saucepan. Add lemon juice and simmer 15 minutes on low heat. Cool in pan.

CARROT NUT CAKE - Pareve

SERVES 10

- 6 eggs, separated
- 1 cup sugar, divided
- 1 cup finely ground walnuts
- 1 cup finely grated carrots
- 1 envelope vanilla sugar
- 1 tsp. each, lemon and orange zest
- 3/4 tsp. cinnamon
- 1/4 tsp. grated nutmeg
- 1 T orange juice
- 3/4 cup matzo cake meal
- 4 T potato starch
  Mocha Coffee Glaze, optional

Preheat oven to 350° F. Set out an ungreased 8" springform pan.

In large bowl of electric mixer, beat egg yolks until light. Gradually add ¾ cup sugar, blend in walnuts, carrots, vanilla sugar, zests of orange, lemon and orange juice. Mix cinnamon and nutmeg with matzo cake meal and potato starch, stir into egg yolk mixture. In clean bowl with clean beaters, beat whites until peaked, gradually add remaining sugar. Beat until stiff, not dry. Fold whites into yolks in three additions.

Scrape batter into pan. Bake 40 to 50 minutes or until cake springs back when lightly touched. Cool 15 minutes in pan, remove sides and bottom to cool completely. Store airtight or freeze. Top with **Mocha Coffee Glaze** (▶see page 126).

APPLE TORTE - Pareve

SERVES 12

- 6 large eggs, separated, room temperature
- 2 cups sugar
- 3/4 cup matzo cake meal
- 3/4 cup potato starch
- 1 cup apple juice
- 1 T freshly grated lemon rind
- 1 tsp. vanilla
- 3 to 4 Granny Smith apples, (1½ lb.) peel, core and thinly slice
- 3/4 tsp. cinnamon
- 1/4 tsp. nutmeg, grated
- 1/2 cup sliced almonds

In large bowl of electric mixer, beat yolks until pale, gradually add 1¾ cups sugar. Beat until very thick. Sift matzo cake meal and potato starch and add to yolks alternately with apple juice. (Begin and end with dry ingredients.) Add rind and vanilla and combine well. In a small bowl, combine 1 T sugar with cinnamon, nutmeg and almonds. Set aside.

Preheat oven to 325° F. Grease a 9 x 13" ovenproof pan.

Wipe a clean bowl with the cut side of a lemon, and with clean beaters, beat whites with a dash of salt until frothy, increase speed and beat until lightly peaked. Add remaining sugar slowly and beat until stiff but not dry. Stir 1 cup of whites into yolk mixture, fold in remaining whites and spread batter in prepared pan. Arrange sliced apples on top of batter and sprinkle with cinnamon sugar mixture and almonds. Bake about 50 minutes until tester comes out clean.

CHOCOLATE RASPBERRY MOUSSE - Pareve

8 PORTIONS

- 1 package frozen raspberries, in syrup, defrosted
- 12 oz. semisweet **or** bittersweet chocolate
- 2 T granulated sugar
- 1/4 cup water
- 6 large eggs, separated room temperature
- 1 tsp. Passover vanilla
- 1 to 2 T Passover brandy, optional
- pinch of salt

In a 1 quart saucepan, simmer raspberries with ½ cup of their syrup until well heated and thickened. Cool. Meanwhile, in microwave or top of double boiler, melt chocolate with sugar and water. Remove from heat, whisk in egg yolks one at a time, and in a slow steady stream, add cooled raspberry sauce to egg yolks mixture. Add vanilla and brandy, if using, pour into a medium bowl, cool.

With mixer on low, in large bowl beat egg whites until foamy, add salt, increase speed to medium high, beat until stiff but not dry. Fold ¼ of beaten whites into chocolate raspberry mixture, gently fold in remaining whites, chill. Spoon into prepared pie shell or serve from a large bowl.

CHOCOLATE CREAM PUFF RING - Pareve

SERVES 8 TO 10

½ cup (1 stick) unsalted pareve margarine, **plus** 1 T to grease pan

1 cup water

1 tsp. sugar

¼ tsp. salt

1 cup matzo cake meal

4 large eggs

Preheat oven to 400° F. Grease a 9" circle on a parchment lined cookie sheet.

In a 2 qt. saucepan, heat margarine, sugar, water and salt. Stir well. Add cake meal all at once. Stir vigorously to form dough into a ball, cool 5 minutes. Beat in eggs one at a time, thoroughly incorporating after each addition.

Drop the batter by the spoonful, touching each other, around the marked circle. Bake 40 minutes until ring is browned and puffed. Cool on rack. Remove from parchment.

CHOCOLATE CREAM FILLING - Pareve

1 cup pareve margarine, room temperature

1 cup granulated sugar

10 oz. bittersweet **or** semi-sweet chocolate

3 large eggs separated, room temperature

1 tsp. Passover vanilla

In large bowl of an electric mixer on medium speed, cream margarine and ½ cup sugar until light and fluffy, about 8 minutes. Meanwhile, melt chocolate in top of double boiler set over hot water or microwave on 50 percent power. Add egg yolks to warm chocolate, stirring constantly until cool. Add chocolate mixture to beaten margarine mixture.

In another clean bowl, with clean beaters, beat egg whites on low speed until foamy. Increase speed to medium and beat until softly peaked, about one minute. Gradually add remaining sugar, a spoonful at a time. Beat until stiff and glossy, about 5 minutes. Fold whites into chocolate mixture in two additions, add vanilla. Chill.

CHOCOLATE GLAZE - Pareve

SERVES 12

4 oz. bittersweet **or** semi-sweet chocolate

2 T sweet unsalted pareve margarine

Assemble two hours before serving. Melt chocolate and margarine over hot water. Keep warm. Slit the ring in half horizontally with a serrated knife. Remove top, fill with chilled chocolate filling, replace top. Drizzle with chocolate glaze before slicing.

Note: MAY BE MADE 8 HOURS AHEAD AND CHILLED. BRING TO ROOM TEMPERATURE BEFORE GLAZING. INDIVIDUAL PUFFS CAN BE MADE AND FILLED SIMILARLY.

In a variation of this recipe, Sephardim make the dough puffs very tiny then deep fry them and drizzle honey on top.

A PASSOVER PAVLOVA - Dairy

SERVES 8 TO 10

unsalted Passover margarine

1 T matzo cake meal

4 egg whites, room temperature

1/2 tsp. salt

1 cup superfine sugar

2 tsp. potato starch

2 tsp. cider vinegar

1 1/2 cups heavy cream, very cold

1/2 tsp. Passover vanilla **or** vanilla sugar

4 kiwi fruit pared, sliced

8 strawberries, hulls intact, rinse, pat dry

Preheat oven to 300° F. Grease a baking sheet and dust with matzo cake meal, shake off excess. Use a pan or template to draw a 7" circle in center of pan with fingertips.

Beat egg whites with salt until softly peaked on low speed of electric mixer. Increase speed to medium, add sugar one tablespoon at a time, beating thoroughly after each addition. Whites will become smooth and glossy. Sift in potato starch and fold into whites. Incorporate vinegar thoroughly.

With rubber spatula, spoon egg whites into center of prepared circle and spread smoothly to edge of circle. Make a slight well about 6" in the middle. Center pan in oven, reduce oven temperature to 250° F. Bake until outside of meringue is firm and pale gold, about one hour and 15 minutes.

Cool meringue on wire rack 15 minutes, loosen carefully from baking sheet with wide, flat spatula. Transfer to serving plate. Let stand uncovered, at room temperature until serving time, about 3 hours maximum.

Whip cream in a large chilled bowl with chilled beaters until stiffly peaked, add vanilla. Spread ¾ of the whipped cream over the well and sides of meringue, leave a slight depression. Overlap kiwi slices around perimeter of meringue.

Spoon remaining whipped cream into pastry bag fitted with a fluted pastry tip. Pipe rosettes in center of meringue and set a strawberry in each rosette. Serve immediately. Cut into 8 or 10 wedges with a serrated knife. Serve with strawberry sauce.

CHOCOLATE MOUSSE CAKE - Pareve

SERVES 10 TO 12

7 oz. semi-sweet chocolate

4 oz. pareve margarine, melted

7 eggs, separated

1 cup vanilla sugar

dash of salt

12 fresh raspberries

Preheat oven to 350°F. Grease a 9" springform pan. Sprinkle with 1 T sugar.

Melt chocolate in microwave on medium power or in top of double boiler set over simmering water. Keep warm.

In a large bowl beat yolks and ¾ cup vanilla sugar until lightened in color and thick. Stir in warm chocolate to slightly cook yolks and add warm margarine.

In a clean bowl, with clean beaters, beat whites with a dash of salt until foamy. Increase speed, add remaining sugar beat until stiff and glossy, but not dry. Fold whites into yolk mixture in three additions. Pour ¾ of batter into prepared pan and bake 35 to 40 minutes. Chill remaining batter.

Cake remains very moist and may fall in the center. Cool completely. Remove from pan, spread remaining batter on top. Chill overnight. When cold, cover with a rigid dome to prevent drying. Garnish with fresh raspberries. Very rich.

HAZELNUT CAKE - Pareve

SERVES 8

1½ cups hazelnuts, finely ground

½ cup hazelnuts, coarsely chopped

½ cup matzo cake meal

2 T Passover confectioners' sugar

1 tsp. grated orange zest

8 T Passover pareve margarine, melted

6 whole eggs, separated

plus 3 egg yolks

1 cup sugar

Preheat oven to 350° F. Toast ground hazelnuts on a baking pan in oven about 3 minutes. Toast chopped hazelnuts until golden, about 5 minutes. Combine the ground hazelnuts with matzo cake meal, confectioner's sugar and orange zest. Set chopped nuts aside.

Grease a 9 x 9" pan with a bit of the margarine, dust with matzo cake meal. Combine confectioners' sugar and orange zest in a small bowl, set aside.

Place eggs, yolks and 1 cup sugar in large metal mixer bowl set over a pan of simmering water. Beat with a whisk or hand beater until warm to the touch, about 7 minutes. Transfer bowl to stand of electric mixer and beat on medium high speed until cool and thickened. Fold in matzo cake meal nut mixture, margarine and chopped hazelnuts. Pour into prepared pan and bake about 40 minutes. Cool on a rack one hour. Invert onto plate. Cake may be frozen if well wrapped. Cut into small squares. Sift with Passover confectioners' sugar.

MATZO MEAL CAKE - Pareve

- 3/4 cup unsalted matzo meal
- 6 eggs, separated, room temperature
- 1 cup sugar
- 3/4 cup chopped walnuts or pecans
- 1 1/2 tsp. Passover baking powder
- 1 tsp. vanilla
- 1/2 tsp. salt
- 1/2 tsp. lemon juice
- 1 tsp. grated lemon zest

Preheat oven to 300° F. Generously grease and flour two 8" round pans.

Briefly refine matzo meal in food processor for one minute. Measure and set aside. Beat yolks in large bowl of electric mixer to blend well. Add 3/4 cup sugar and beat until light in color and doubled in volume. Slowly stir in matzo meal, baking powder, vanilla, lemon zest and salt.

Rub a clean bowl with the lemon juice. Beat whites with a dash of salt until foamy, increase speed, beat until peaked. Slowly add remaining sugar and beat until stiff, but not dry. Fold whites into matzo meal mixture in several additions.

Divide batter between pans and bake until tester comes out clean, about 50 minutes.

Cool briefly, turn onto racks until completely cool.

Note: CAKE MAY BE BAKED, WRAPPED IN PLASTIC AND FROZEN. DEFROST AND THEN MAKE VANILLA GLAZE.

- 1 cup Passover confectioners' sugar
- 1/2 tsp. potato starch
- 1 tsp. vanilla
- 1 to 3 T hot water
- 1 T Passover wine **or** brandy
- 1/2 cup Passover cherry preserves
- 1/4 cup chopped nuts

Vanilla Sugar Glaze

Combine ingredients for vanilla sugar glaze. Stir to make a spreadable mixture. Spread a thin layer of glaze on flat sides of layers. Place one layer on platter and top with preserves, place second layer on top. Spread remaining glaze over top and let drip down side. Garnish with nuts.

PASSOVER PIES and BROWNIES

MATZO MEAL PIE CRUST - Pareve

SERVES 8 TO 10

1/4 cup unsalted pareve
     Passover margarine
 2   T sugar
     dash of salt
1/2 tsp. ground cinnamon
 1   cup matzo meal
 1   tsp. potato starch
1/4 cup ground walnuts
 2   T red Passover wine

Preheat oven to 350° F. Lightly grease a 9 or 10" pie plate.

In a medium mixing bowl, cream margarine, sugar, salt and cinnamon. Slowly add matzo meal, potato starch and walnuts. Add enough wine to bind the mixture. Press into pie plate with fingers or a wooden spoon.

Bake in the center of the oven for 10 to 12 minutes. Cool. Fill as desired. Store in refrigerator.

Note: IF USING WITH A FILLING TO BE BAKED, BAKE PIE CRUST 5 TO 6 MINUTES.

COCONUT MACAROON PIE SHELL - Pareve

 2   cups sweetened coconut
     flakes
 2   T matzo cake meal
 1   tsp. potato starch
     dash of salt
 2   large egg whites,
     room temperature
1/3 cup sugar

Preheat oven to 375° F. Generously spray a 9" springform pan with vegetable spray. Line with parchment paper, spray again (not necessary on a non-stick pan). Set aside.

Mix together coconut, matzo cake meal, potato starch and salt in a bowl. Lightly beat egg whites with a fork, add sugar and beat until thickened. Stir into coconut mixture.

Press mixture into prepared pan. Bake about 15 to 20 minutes. Reduce heat to 350° F. Bake another 5 minutes if macaroon shell is not set. Cool. Remove sides of pan, fill with chocolate or lemon mousse. Keep refrigerated.

LEMON MOUSSE PIE - Pareve

SERVES 8 TO 10

coconut macaroon pie shell, baked

6 eggs, separated, room temperature

1 1/2 cups sugar, divided

1/2 cup **plus** 2 T lemon juice

2 T grated lemon zest

2 packets unflavored kosher gelatin

pinch of salt

mint leaves

In 2 qt. heavy saucepan, whisk egg yolks, add 1 1/4 cups sugar, 1/2 cup lemon juice and zest. Place pan over medium low heat, stir 4 minutes until mixture begins to thicken. DO NOT BOIL.

When mixture is at pudding consistency, add lemon zest, pour into a bowl. Cover with plastic wrap, piercing the plastic so steam escapes. Cool slightly.

In a large clean bowl of electric mixer with clean beaters, beat egg whites and salt on medium speed until softly peaked. Increase speed, slowly add remaining 1/4 cup sugar, beating until stiff, not dry. Fold whites into warm lemon mixture in three additions. Dissolve gelatin in the 2 T lemon juice, warm slightly to dissolve, add gelatin to the lemon mousse.

Pour batter into prepared coconut crust in springform pan. Cover and chill several hours or overnight. Remove sides of pan, cut into wedges and garnish with mint leaves.

LOW-FAT COTTAGE CHEESE PIE FILLING - Dairy

MAKES 8 PORTIONS

one prepared 10" matzo meal pie crust, unbaked

8 oz. low-fat cottage cheese, pressed through a sieve

8 oz. low-fat cream cheese, softened

2 whole eggs, separated

2 egg whites, room temperature

2/3 cup sugar

1 cup low fat sour cream

1 1/2 T potato starch

1 T freshly grated orange zest

1 tsp. vanilla
or 1 T vanilla sugar

Preheat oven to 325° F. In large bowl of electric mixer, beat the cottage cheese and cream cheese. Add yolks one at a time. Add all but 2T sugar, sour cream, potato starch, orange zest, vanilla and blend well.

In another clean bowl with clean beaters, beat egg whites until foamy, add salt. Add 2 T sugar, beat until stiffly peaked. Fold whites into the cheese mixture in two additions.

Spoon into prepared crust, bake in center of oven for 45 to 50 minutes, until set. Turn oven off and allow pie to cool in pan, loosely tented with aluminum foil for several hours. Chill several hours or overnight. Garnish with fresh berries.

FIG and YOGURT CHEESE PIE - Dairy

SERVES 8

one fully baked and cooled matzo meal pie crust.

2 cups stiff yogurt cheese

3/4 cup (5 oz.) good quality figs, chopped

1/3 cup honey

1 1/2 tsp. vanilla
or 1 T vanilla sugar

grated zest of one lemon

1 T Passover orange marmalade

1/4 cup chopped walnuts, for garnish

Filling

Prepare yogurt cheese one day ahead. Spoon 1 qt. plain yogurt into a sieve lined with cheesecloth or double paper towels. Place sieve over a bowl or pie plate and cover with plastic wrap. Drain in refrigerator overnight. Yields 2 cups yogurt cheese to use many ways. Yogurt cheese keeps 5 days refrigerated.

In a small saucepan, combine chopped figs, honey and boiling water to cover. Bring to a boil, reduce heat, simmer and stir occasionally for 10 minutes. Cover until remaining liquid is absorbed and thickens, about 20 minutes.

Stir fig mixture, vanilla and lemon zest into yogurt cheese. Brush the pie shell with 1 T orange marmalade. Spoon filling into prepared crust and sprinkle with walnuts. Chill 30 minutes. When set, cover with plastic wrap. Chill several hours or overnight.

STRAWBERRY YOGURT CHEESE PIE - Dairy

Prepare yogurt cheese as above. Mix 3 T strawberry jelly instead of figs with remaining ingredients. Brush another 2 T strawberry jam on prepared pie crust. Pour the strawberry yogurt cheese into pie shell and chill. Serve decorated with dollops of drained low-fat strawberry yogurt and fresh strawberries. Keep chilled.

BROWNIE PIE - Pareve

SERVES 10

1 cup finely chopped walnuts

6 to 8 T matzo meal

3 T sugar

1/2 tsp. cinnamon

4 T melted Passover margarine

Crust

Preheat oven to 375° F. Lightly grease a 10" pie plate.

In a medium bowl, combine all crust ingredients. They should hold together when pinched between the fingers. Press into pie pan. Bake crust 5 to 8 minutes, until set.

Fill a partially baked crust with the first **brownie recipe** (▶see page 138). Reduce oven to 350° F and bake 35 to 40 minutes. A knife inserted in center will come out clean. Cool on a rack. Cut in wedges to serve. Brownie pie keeps well overnight covered with plastic or frozen.

Note: TO USE CRUST WITH AN UNBAKED FILLING, BAKE 10 TO 12 MINUTES UNTIL GOLDEN AND FIRM.

RICH BROWNIES I - Pareve

- 6 oz. semi-sweet chocolate cut up
- 1 cup (2 sticks) unsalted pareve margarine
- 4 eggs, room temperature
  pinch of salt
- 1¼ cups sugar
- ½ tsp. vanilla
  or 1 T vanilla sugar
- 1 cup matzo cake meal
- 1 cup chopped walnuts

Preheat oven to 350° F. Grease a 9 x 13" baking pan, dust with matzo cake flour.

Melt chocolate and margarine in microwave at 50 percent power or in top of double boiler set over hot water. Cool.

Beat eggs with a pinch of salt, add sugar, beat until thick and lemon-colored. Blend in cooled chocolate mixture, vanilla and cake meal. Stir in ⅔ cup nuts. Pour into prepared pan, smooth with rubber spatula. Sprinkle top with remaining nuts. Bake 30 to 35 minutes. Cool on a rack, cut into squares while slightly warm.

Note: TO FILL BROWNIE PIE, REDUCE NUTS TO ¾ CUP. ADD ½ CUP NUTS TO BATTER AND SPRINKLE ¼ CUP ON TOP OF PIE BEFORE BAKING.

BROWNIES II - Pareve

MAKES 24 SQUARES

- 4 large eggs
- 2 scant cups sugar
- 1 tsp. Passover vanilla
  or 1 T vanilla sugar
- ¾ cup vegetable oil
- 8 T cocoa
- ½ cup black coffee
- 1 cup matzo cake meal, sifted
- 2 T potato starch
- ¾ cup chopped walnuts

Preheat oven to 350° F. Grease a 9 x 13" pan, dust with cake meal.

Beat eggs and sugar until thick. Add vanilla, oil, cocoa and black coffee. Slowly add matzo cake meal and potato starch. Stir in ½ cup nuts. Pour batter into pan, smooth top. Sprinkle with remaining nuts.

Bake about 30 to 35 minutes until a knife inserted in center comes out clean. Cool in pan on a rack. Cut into squares while warm. This recipe is lower in fat. Store airtight.

LOW-FAT BROWNIES - Pareve

MAKES 16 SQUARES

- 1/2 cup vegetable oil **plus** 1 tsp. vegetable oil or spray
- 1 cup sugar
- 3 large egg whites, lightly beaten
- dash of salt
- 1/2 cup matzo cake meal
- 1/3 cup cocoa
- 1/3 cup walnuts, chopped

Preheat oven to 325° F. Grease an 8 x 8" pan with vegetable oil or spray, lightly dust with matzo cake meal.

In large bowl of electric mixer, beat oil and sugar together. Add lightly beaten egg whites with a dash of salt and incorporate well. Sift matzo cake meal and cocoa together, add to batter; stir in nuts.

Scrape batter into prepared pan, bake 20 to 25 minutes. Cool briefly and cut while warm.

Note: RECIPE CAN BE DOUBLED. BAKE IN A 9 X 13" PAN ABOUT 30 TO 35 MINUTES. COVER WELL AND CHILL, DO NOT FREEZE.

APPLE RHUBARB CRISP - Pareve

8 PORTIONS

- 1/4 cup matzo meal
- 1/2 cup matzo cake meal
- 2/3 cup packed brown sugar
- 3 T sugar
- 1/4 cup finely chopped toasted almonds **or** walnuts
- 1/2 tsp. ground cinnamon
- 1/8 tsp. ground nutmeg
- 8 T Passover margarine, slightly softened, cut into pieces

Topping

Combine all topping ingredients in a bowl, work in butter until mixture resembles coarse meal. It should just hold together, but be crumbly.

- 2 lb. baking apples
- 1 1/2 lb. rhubarb
- 1 to 1 1/2 cups sugar
- 3 T matzo cake meal
- 1 T potato starch
- 1 tsp. ground cinnamon

Filling

Preheat oven to 350° F. Peel, core and quarter apples, cut quarters into four chunks for about 5 cups. Trim rhubarb and cut into 1" x ½" pieces for about 5 cups. In a large bowl, toss apples, rhubarb, sugar, matzo cake meal, potato starch, cinnamon and nutmeg until well coated. Transfer to a 2 qt. casserole and sprinkle the topping over. Bake until golden brown and fruit is bubbling, 1 hour to 1¼ hours. Serve warm. Can be refrigerated or frozen. Reheat in a 300° F oven.

FRUIT DESSERTS

STRAWBERRIES in STRAWBERRIES -
Pareve

SERVES 8

1 pkg. (16 oz.) frozen strawberries

2 T orange juice

1 tsp. lemon juice

1 T sweet red wine

1 qt. fresh strawberries

fresh mint leaves to garnish, if available

Process frozen strawberries, juices and red wine until smooth. Chill in a glass serving bowl. To serve, rinse and halve or slice fresh berries into the sauce. Garnish with mint leaves. Serve with cookies.

FRESH CITRUS and BERRIES - Pareve

SERVES 8 TO 10

6 navel oranges

2 pink grapefruit

1 1/2 cups grated unsweetened coconut

1 cup sugar

2 T white Passover wine

2 kiwi fruit

1/2 pint raspberries

Rinse oranges and grapefruit under boiling water briefly. Peel and thinly slice oranges and grapefruit over a bowl; save juices. Alternate layers of sliced fruit and coconut in a glass bowl. Lightly sprinkle each layer with sugar. Pour wine and juices over fruit and chill. Slice the kiwi fruit on top and garnish with raspberries.

APPLESAUCE - Pareve

MAKES 1 1-2 QTS

3 lbs. cooking apples

1 cup apple juice

dash of salt

3/4 cup sugar, or to taste

1/2 tsp. cinnamon

dash of nutmeg

Cut apples into quarters, remove core. Cut quarters into chunks and place in a 4 qt. pot. Add the apple juice and a dash of salt. Cover pot and bring to a simmer. Cook about 20 minutes until apples are very tender and most of the juice is absorbed. Cool until easy to handle.

Press apples through a food mill or coarse sieve into a 2 qt. bowl. Add cinnamon and sugar to taste. Store in a glass bowl covered with plastic in refrigerator. Serve with matzo meal pancakes or as a side dish.

ORANGE SLICES with MOROCCAN SPICES - Pareve

SERVES 10 TO 12

- 10 Jaffa oranges
- 2 T orange flower water, optional
- 8 T sugar
- 2 limes
- 1 lemon
- 6 sprigs fresh mint
- 1/2 lb. pitted dates

  pinches of Moroccan spices (recipe below)

  Passover Confectioner's sugar

With a zester, remove zest from two oranges, reserve. Peel oranges, remove all membrane; separate into segments or slice. Place in a serving bowl. Squeeze any juice over orange segments to keep moist. Add orange flower water and one tablespoon of sugar. Chill oranges one hour or longer.

Remove thin strips of zest from limes and lemon. Blanch all zests in boiling water 1 minute, drain, rinse in cold water, pat dry.

Place remaining sugar and 1 cup water in small saucepan. Heat, stirring until sugar dissolves. Boil 30 seconds and add the three zests. Lower heat, stir once and simmer slowly until zest is very soft, about 5 minutes. Do not allow syrup to caramelize. Lift and separate zests on an oiled cookie rack to dry.

To serve, shred mint leaves, chop dates. Scatter mint, dates and pinches of the spice mixture on oranges. Decorate with candied zests and a dusting of confectioner's sugar.

- 3/4 tsp. ground nutmeg
- 1/4 tsp. cloves
- 1 tsp. freshly ground black pepper
- 1 tsp. freshly ground white pepper
- 13/4 tsp. ground cinnamon
- 2 tsp. ground cardamom
- 1/4 tsp. cayenne pepper

Moroccan Spices

Combine all spices and process until finely ground. Press through a sieve. Keep airtight in a glass jar. Use on any fruits and vegetables

STRAWBERRY SAUCE - Pareve

MAKES 2 CUPS

- 1 pt. strawberries
- 2 T sweet red wine
- 6 T sugar, more or less according to sweetness of berries

Combine 1 pt. strawberries, 2 T red wine and 2 T sugar in a bowl. Allow to macerate 30 minutes. Puree in food processor until smooth. Make raspberry sauce similarly, except press raspberries through a fine sieve to remove seeds. Keep sauces refrigerated up to 10 days.

PEPPERY FRESH PINEAPPLE SLICES -
Pareve or Dairy

SERVES 8

1 or 2   whole fresh, ripe pineapples

4 to 6   T pareve unsalted margarine

2   T freshly grated black pepper or to taste

1/2   pint fresh raspberries

Option: Vanilla yogurt or 1 recipe **mock whipped cream** (▶see page 155)

Peel, core and cut pineapple crosswise into ½" slices. Grind black pepper over the slices. Melt 1 T margarine in a non-stick skillet. Sauté pineapple slices in batches, adding extra margarine as needed. Rinse and pick over raspberries. Remove to individual plates, garnish with raspberries and pass the "whipped cream."

RASPBERRY POACHED PEARS - Pareve

SERVES 8

1 1/4   cups sugar

4   long strips of lemon zest

1   package (8 oz.) frozen raspberries

8   firm but ripe Bosc pears

fresh mint leaves to garnish

1/2   pint raspberries, picked over

In a large saucepan that holds pears in a single layer, bring sugar and 4 cups water to a boil. Stir to dissolve sugar, add lemon zest and simmer 10 minutes.

Meanwhile, puree frozen raspberries in a processor. Press through a fine sieve to remove seeds. Stir into the syrup and remove from heat. Can be made one day in advance and chilled.

Peel pears and remove core through base with a vegetable peeler. Keep stems in place if desired. Bring syrup to a simmer and add pears. Cook, turning several times for about 30 minutes, until still tender but firm.

Transfer to a serving bowl with a slotted spoon. Reduce syrup by one-third and strain over the pears, chill. Garnish with fresh mint leaves and fresh raspberries.

ROASTED PEARS in HONEY - Pareve

MAKES 8 PORTIONS

- 4 large pears, peeled, cored and halved
- 2 tsp. unsalted pareve margarine
- 1/2 cup honey
- 2 whole cloves
- 1/2 cup sliced almonds

A delicious low fat dessert I use year-round.

Preheat oven to 325° F. Toast almonds on a sheet of foil 10 minutes, until golden.

Melt margarine in a large heavy cast-iron skillet on medium heat. Add pears, cook until caramelized, 3 to 5 minutes per side. Reduce heat, add honey and cloves. When honey melts, turn pears to coat both sides. Cover and cook about 5 to 10 minutes, until tender.

Partially slice pear halves from wide end but not through narrow end. Fan out on a plate. Spoon honey sauce over each pear, scatter almonds on top. Serve warm or at room temperature. Serve with blue cheese at a dairy meal. (Recipe doubles easily.)

BAKED PEAR CASSEROLE - Pareve

SERVES 6 TO 8

- 6 firm ripe Bosc pears, (2 1/2 lb.)
- 1 T fresh lemon juice
- 1 cup matzo meal
- 1/3 cup light brown sugar
- 1/4 cup granulated sugar
- 1/2 tsp. cinnamon
- 1/4 tsp. grated nutmeg
- 3 T unsalted Passover margarine, cut up

Preheat oven to 375° F. Grease a 9" pie plate or shallow casserole.

Peel, quarter and slice pears crosswise, about 1/2 inch thick. In medium bowl, toss pears in lemon juice. In a small bowl, combine matzo meal, the sugars and spices.

Spread 2 T of matzo meal mixture in prepared pan, cover with half the pears. Drizzle with 2 T of water, scatter about half the remaining crumb mixture over pears, dot with margarine. Add remaining pears, sprinkle with crumb mixture and dot with margarine. Set dish on a baking sheet. Bake about 40 minutes, until pears are tender. Cool.

Option: GARNISH WITH RASPBERRIES.

MELON COMPOTE with TOASTED ALMONDS - Pareve

MAKES 6 PORTIONS

- 3 cups cantaloupe chunks
- 3 cups honeydew chunks
- 1/4 cup fresh lime juice
- 3 T sugar
- 1/2 tsp. freshly ground nutmeg, optional
- 1 cup seedless green grapes
- 1/4 cup almonds, lightly toasted, optional

Combine melons, lime juice and 2 T sugar in a bowl. Gently toss to coat well. Chill. Combine 1 T sugar and the nutmeg and gently stir into the melon compote. Scatter grapes and almonds on top.

DRIED FRUIT COMPOTE - Pareve

MAKES 1 1/2 QUARTS

- 8 oz. pitted prunes
- 1 package (12 oz.) mixed dried fruits
- 1/2 cup golden raisins
- 1/4 cup dried currants
- 2 1/2 cups weak tea
- 2 cups red wine
- 3/4 cup white sugar
- 1/4 cup brown sugar
- 2 whole cloves
- 1 stick cinnamon
- 2 T Passover brandy **or** liqueur, optional

Combine fruits and tea in a 2 qt. saucepan, bring to a simmer on medium heat for 10 minutes. Set aside to intensify flavor for several hours. Meanwhile, combine vinegar and sugars in heavy saucepan over medium heat. Swirl to dissolve sugars, add spices and boil 10 minutes. Cool.

Drain fruits and place in a glass bowl, strain syrup over fruits. Discard spices. Keep at room temperature 24 hours. Strain syrup into saucepan and boil for 10 minutes, add brandy.

Pour syrup over fruit in glass bowl or jar with airtight lid, cover and set aside in dark cupboard to steep for several days. Chill. Keeps 2 weeks, refrigerated.

APPLE NUT RING - Pareve

SERVES 8

1/4 cup matzo cake meal

1/2 cup matzo meal

3/4 cup walnuts, chopped

2 T brown sugar

1 tsp. cinnamon

10 to 12 Red Delicious apples

4 T cold unsalted pareve
margarine, cut up

1/4 cup softened golden
raisins, optional

1/2 cup white wine

6 T sugar

Preheat oven to 375° F. Grease a 10 x 2" deep round quiche or pie pan with 1 tsp. margarine.

Process matzo cake meal and matzo meal in processor bowl with walnuts, brown sugar, and cinnamon until nuts are finely ground. Place nut mixture on a sheet of waxed paper.

Peel and cut apples in half. Core and thinly slice each half crosswise. Toss in bowl with lemon juice to prevent discoloration.

Press apple slices into nut mixture, stand in concentric circles, rounded side up in the pan. Fill in between slices and mound extra slices in center. Dot with margarine. Pour remaining crumb mixture on top.

Cover with foil and cut a steam vent in center of foil. Bake 30 minutes. Heat wine, stir in sugar to dissolve. Uncover apples, reduce heat to 350° F, scatter raisins and pour wine mixture over apples. Bake until apples are golden and juices are thick and bubbly. Serve warm or at room temperature.

NUTRIENT ANALYSIS

Total Calories: 212	Fat: 7g (26%)	Carbohydrate: 37g (65%)
Cholesterol: 0mg	Protein: 3g (6%)	Alcohol: 1g (3 %)

STRAWBERRY RHUBARB SAUCE - Pareve

1 cup sugar

1/2 cup water

1 tsp. vanilla or vanilla sugar

1 tsp. lemon juice

dash of salt

1 1/2 lb. fresh rhubarb, cut in
1" pieces
or 1 bag unsweetened
rhubarb, frozen (20 oz.)

1 qt. fresh
or 1 package unsweetened
frozen strawberries

In a 3 qt. saucepan, bring sugar and water to a boil, simmer 5 minutes until sugar dissolves. Add vanilla, lemon juice, salt and rhubarb pieces. Return to a simmer, cover and cook until rhubarb is tender, about 15 minutes. Add sliced fresh berries or defrosted packaged berries directly from bag. Cook about 5 minutes, until fruit is very soft. Cool.

Pour into a glass bowl, cover and refrigerate several hours or overnight. Garnish with curls of lemon zest or mint sprigs. Serve on Passover cakes or with cookies

BAKED APPLES with ISRAELI FRUITS and MACAROONS - Pareve

8 SERVINGS

- 3 T golden raisins
- 1 tea bag
- 8 medium baking apples, about 2¹/2 lb.
- 1 lemon, halved
- 3 T dried apricots, chopped
- 3 T each, dried figs and dates, chopped
- 3 T blanched slivered almonds
- 4 T sugar
- 1¹/2 T margarine
- 3 T dry white wine
- 4 macaroons

Preheat oven to 375° F. Line a non-corrosive baking pan with parchment paper.

Soak raisins in 1 cup strong hot tea 15 minutes. Slice off top third of apples, rub cut portions with lemon. Remove core, widen center to hold stuffing and leave ¹/2 inch at bottom. Trim apples to stand securely. Cover with wax paper.

Drain raisins, pat dry, combine with apricots, dates and figs. Crumble macaroons, add with almonds to fruits. Heat white wine and sugar until sugar dissolves. Set apples in pan. Spoon fruit mixture into apple centers, add a spoon of wine mixture to each apple. Dot with a dab of margarine, replace tops.

Bake 30 to 35 minutes, until tender but apples retain their shape. Serve warm or chilled.

NUTRITIOAL ANALYSIS

Total Calories: 314	Fat: 5g (14%)	Carbohydrate: 69g (81%)		
Cholesterol: 0mg	Protein: 2g (3%)	Alcohol: 7g (3 %)		Fiber: 6g

COCONUT MACAROON CUPCAKES - Pareve

12 SERVINGS

- 4 egg whites, room temperature
- pinch of salt
- ¹/2 cup sugar
- 1¹/2 cup shredded sweetened coconut
- ¹/4 cup sugar
- ¹/4 cup ground blanched almonds
- 2 T matzo cake meal
- ¹/2 tsp. grated lemon rind

Preheat oven to 350° F. Line a twelve section muffin tin with paper muffin cups.

Beat egg whites with a pinch of salt until they hold soft peaks, gradually beat in ¹/2 cup sugar. Beat until the meringue holds stiff peaks and is smooth and shiny. In another bowl, combine the shredded coconut, ¹/2 cup sugar, the almonds, matzo cake meal and grated lemon rind. Gently fold the mixture into the meringue.

Fill prepared muffin cups ¾ full of batter. Bake 20 to 25 minutes until golden brown and crusty on the surface. Store airtight several days.

SORBET

LEMON SORBET - Pareve

MAKES 2½ CUPS

1½ cups sugar
 2   cups water
⅓   cup lemon juice
½   an egg white

In a saucepan over medium high heat, dissolve sugar in water and boil 5 minutes. Remove from heat and stir in the lemon juice. Cool slightly, pour through a fine sieve. When nearly cool, whisk in the egg white. Freeze until slushy.

Spoon into the processor and blend until mixture is creamy and light in color. Freeze in the processor bowl and blend again when nearly frozen. Spoon into a freezer container or lemon shells. Freeze.

ORANGE SORBET - Pareve

MAKES 6 CUPS

 2   scant cups sugar
 1   cup water
 4   cups freshly squeezed
     orange juice
¾   cup lemon juice
 1   egg white
 1   T finely grated orange zest
 6   oranges
     mint leaves

Cook sugar and water in a two-quart saucepan on medium heat, stirring until sugar dissolves. Continue to boil until mixture is thick and syrupy. Remove from heat and pour into an 8 cup measuring cup. Add orange and lemon juices, freeze until slushy.

In a small bowl, beat egg white until stiff but not dry. Fold into the juice and freeze until firm. Spoon into the processor bowl and blend until creamy and light in color. Spoon into freezer container, cover and freeze until firm.

Cut oranges in half and scoop out the pulp. Save for another use. Trim ends to stand firmly. Fill the shells with orange sorbet. Freeze. Garnish with mint leaves.

STRAWBERRY SORBET - Pareve

MAKES 2 CUPS

 1   quart strawberries
½   cup sugar
 1   T lemon juice
 1   egg white

Process strawberries, sugar and lemon juice until smooth. Freeze two hours in processor bowl. Return bowl to stand of processor, activate. Add egg white and process until smooth. Spoon into a freezer container. Keep frozen until serving.

Note: ALL SORBET ARE PAREVE.

COOKIES

PASSOVER RUSSIAN TEA BISCUITS - Pareve

from Ellen Petler

MAKES 3 DOZEN

1 cup sugar
1/4 tsp. salt
4 T potato starch
2 cups matzo cake meal
2 T orange juice
  grated orange zest
4 eggs
2/3 cup vegetable oil
  Passover raspberry preserves
1 cup golden raisins
1/2 cup chopped walnuts
1 egg white
  cinnamon sugar

Sift dry ingredients into a large bowl. Make a well in the center, add eggs and oil. Oil or wet hands and knead dough. Wrap in plastic and chill at least two hours.

Preheat oven to 325° F. Oil 2 baking sheets.

Divide dough into quarters. Roll one piece of dough between sheets of wax paper. Spread dough with preserves, sprinkle with nuts and raisins. Roll from long side. Brush roll with egg white and sprinkle with cinnamon and sugar. Slice and place on an oiled cookie sheet. Repeat with remaining dough. Bake 30 to 35 minutes. Cool on rack. May be frozen.

PECAN COOKIES - Pareve

MAKES ABOUT 4 DOZEN

1/2 cup (1 stick) unsalted pareve margarine, softened
1 cup sugar
2 whole eggs **plus** 2 whites
1 1/2 cups finely chopped pecans
1 cup matzo cake meal
1 T lemon **or** orange juice
  vegetable oil **or** spray
1/2 cup pecan pieces

A favorite from my Aunt Fanny Myeroff

❖ ❖ ❖

Preheat oven to 350° F. Spray 2 cookie sheets with vegetable oil spray.

Cream margarine and sugar, add eggs one at a time and egg whites. Stir in nuts, cake meal and fruit juice.

Drop by the rounded teaspoonful onto cookie sheets. Top each cookie with pecan pieces. Bake about 8 minutes until golden. Cool on a rack. Store airtight and out of sight or they disappear!

CHOCOLATE CHIP COOKIES - Pareve

4 DOZEN COOKIES

1   cup granulated sugar

½   cup brown sugar

½   cup pareve unsalted margarine

½   tsp. Passover baking soda

½   tsp. vanilla
    or 1 T vanilla sugar

2   large eggs, room temperature

¾   cup matzo cake meal, sifted

¼   cup matzo meal, sifted

¼   cup potato starch, sifted

¼   cup water

1   cup Passover chocolate chips

½   cup walnuts, chopped

The kids love these.

Preheat oven to 350° F. Grease or spray 2 cookie sheets.

In a large bowl of electric mixer, cream the sugars, margarine, baking soda and vanilla until light and fluffy. Add eggs one at a time, blend well. Add sifted dry ingredients and enough water to make a smooth cohesive batter. Stir in chocolate chips and walnuts with a wooden spoon.

Drop by the teaspoonful onto prepared cookie sheets. Bake about 12 minutes or until firm and golden. Cool on a rack.

CHOCOLATE BAR COOKIES - Pareve

3   eggs

1   cup sugar

½   cup vegetable oil

½   tsp. Passover vanilla

3   T orange juice

1   cup semi-sweet chocolate, grated

½   cup chopped nuts

2   tsp. grated orange zest

2   cups matzo meal

¼   tsp. salt

2   T cocoa

Preheat oven to 350° F. Grease a 9 x 13 x 1" baking sheet.

Beat eggs and sugar until thick and lemon colored, add oil, vanilla and orange juice. Stir in chopped nuts, grated chocolate, orange zest and salt. Blend in matzo meal.

Pour into pan, smooth with rubber spatula. Bake 20 to 25 minutes. Cool, cut into 24 bars while warm. Store or freeze airtight. Dust with cocoa or spread with chocolate glaze.

LEMON SQUARES - Pareve

MAKES 16 SQUARES

- 1/2 cup matzo cake meal
- 1/4 cup potato starch
- 1/4 tsp. salt
- 1/2 cup vegetable oil
- 2/3 cup sugar
- 3 T finely grated lemon zest
- 3 T lemon juice
- 1 T orange juice
- 1/2 cup walnuts, chopped
- 2 large egg whites, lightly beaten
- 4 T sugar mixed with 1/2 tsp. cinnamon

Preheat oven to 350° F. Spray a 9" square pan with vegetable spray.

Sift cake meal, potato starch and salt together, set aside. In the large bowl of an electric mixer, beat oil and sugar on medium speed 3 minutes. Add lemon zest and sifted dry ingredients alternately with lemon and orange juices. Stir in chopped walnuts with a wooden spoon.

In another clean bowl with a clean whisk beater, beat egg whites until foamy, increase speed to medium high and continue beating until softly peaked. Fold into lemon mixture and blend well. Scrape batter in prepared pan. Bake 25 to 30 minutes, until set.

While hot, cut into 2" squares. Sprinkle with cinnamon sugar mixture. Cool completely.

FARFEL COOKIES - Pareve

MAKES ABOUT 48

- 1/2 cup chopped almonds, toasted
- 1/2 cup golden raisins
- 1 cup matzo meal
- 1 cup matzo farfel
- 1 scant cup sugar
- 2 large eggs
- 1/3 cup vegetable oil
- 1/2 tsp. cinnamon

Here's two great recipes to make with the children.

Preheat oven to 350° F. Lightly grease or spray 2 cookie sheets.

On a sheet of foil, toast almonds in oven until golden, about 5 minutes. Cool, coarsely chop and set aside. Soften raisins in hot water 15 minutes, drain and pat dry.

In large bowl, combine matzo meal, farfel, sugar and half the toasted almonds. With a wooden spoon, add eggs and oil, combine well with dry ingredients. Add cinnamon, raisins.

Drop by the teaspoon onto prepared cookie sheets. Center a few almonds on each cookie mound. Bake 20 to 25 minutes. Cool on a rack. Store airtight.

LAYERED MATZO COOKIES - Pareve

MAKES 12 PIECES

6 T sugar
4 oz. semi-sweet chocolate
1 cup **plus** 2 T water
7 T pareve unsalted margarine
6 oz. halvah, cut up
1/2 cup Passover sweet red wine
2 T potato starch
6 sheets matzo
1 oz. semi-sweet chocolate
   to grate on top

In a medium saucepan, melt chocolate, sugar and 1 cup water. Bring just to a simmer on low heat, stir until melted and smooth. Add margarine piece by piece, halvah and wine. Stir to return mixture to a boil, remove from heat. Combine potato starch and 2 T water, stir into chocolate. Heat until blended.

Place one sheet of matzo on a piece of foil, spread with 3 T chocolate. Continue layering matzo and chocolate, finish with chocolate. Grate remaining chocolate on top. Chill. Cut into squares place on a serving dish.

DATE and NUT BARS - Pareve

MAKES 12 SQUARES

3 eggs
1/2 cup sugar
3/4 cup chopped dates
3 T matzo cake meal
1 cup chopped walnuts
1/4 cup fresh orange juice
1 T grated orange zest

Preheat oven to 350°F. Grease a 9" square pan.

Beat eggs and sugar until thick and light in color. Dust chopped dates with matzo cake meal. Add to batter with remaining ingredients. Spread in the pan and bake 30 minutes. Cut into squares while warm. (Freezes well.)

ALMOND MERINGUE COOKIES - Pareve

MAKES 48 COOKIES

1 cup chopped almonds
3 extra large egg whites
1/8 tsp. salt
2/3 cup sugar

Preheat oven to 300° F; line 2 cookie sheets with parchment paper.

Finely grind almonds in bowl of food processor, set aside. In large bowl of electric mixer with whisk beater on medium speed, beat whites and salt until frothy, increase speed to medium high, slowly add sugar, beat until stiff but not dry. Blend in ground nuts.

Drop by the teaspoonful onto prepared baking sheets. Bake 40 to 45 minutes, switching pans after 20 minutes, until golden and crisp. Cool on racks. Store airtight.

MOLDED CARAMEL MOUSSE - Pareve

SERVES 12

12	large egg whites, room temperature
2³/4	cups sugar
	dash of lemon juice
	pinch of salt
	fresh flowers
	mint leaves

Preheat oven to 250°F. Grease a 3 quart ovenproof mold and dust with 1 T sugar. In a heavy 10" skillet set over medium high heat, cook ¾ cup sugar with a squeeze of lemon juice until golden.

Meanwhile, in large bowl of electric mixer on low speed, beat whites until foamy, 1 minute. Add salt, increase speed to medium high, beating until softly peaked. Gradually add remaining 2 cups sugar, 1 tablespoon at a time. Beat until stiff and glossy, 5 to 10 minutes.

Keep syrup hot and fluid until whites are stiff. In a slow steady stream, pour syrup into whites, beating constantly. Do not allow hot syrup to touch beaters or bowl. Continue beating until meringue is cool to the touch and thick, about 10 minutes.

With rubber spatula, scrape into prepared casserole and place in a larger pan. Add enough hot water to reach ⅓ of the way up the casserole. Bake until firm, about 1 hour. Cool. Chill overnight.

To unmold, place platter over mold, invert and cover with a hot towel. Remove towel and gently shake mousse. If it does not release, loosen at one side with knife to get some air beneath the mold. Invert on serving platter. Decorate with fresh flowers and mint leaves.

GLAZED PECANS - Pareve

¹/4	cup sugar
12	pecan halves

Oil a baking sheet. Heat sugar in a small heavy skillet on low heat. Stir until sugar dissolves. Cook until syrup is golden. Stir in pecans and coat well. Cool on baking sheet.

CHOCOLATE MERINGUE PUFFS -
Pareve - Low-Fat

MAKES 24 PUFFS

- 4 egg whites, room temperature
  dash of salt
- 3/4 cup sugar
- 4 T cocoa powder
  almond slices, optional

Preheat oven to 300° F. Lightly grease a baking pan, line with parchment paper and lightly grease again.

Beat egg whites until foamy, add a dash of salt. Gradually increase speed, slowly add sugar until batter is glossy and stiff, but not dry. Fold in cocoa powder. Fill pastry bag, or use two teaspoons to drop onto prepared baking sheet. Top with almond slices. Bake about 30 to 45 minutes until meringues appear dry and set. Store airtight.

MACAROONS - Pareve

MAKES 3 DOZEN

- 4 egg whites
  dash of salt
- 1 cup sugar
- 1/2 tsp. vanilla
- 3 cups shredded unsweetened coconut

Preheat oven to 375° F. Set out two ungreased cookie sheets.

Beat egg whites in large bowl of electric mixer with a dash of salt on low speed. Gradually increase to medium high speed and slowly add sugar. Beat until stiff but not dry. Fold in vanilla and coconut. Drop by the spoonful onto cookie sheets, flatten tops.

Bake 15 minutes, until golden. Cool on a rack, store airtight.

CHOCOLATE ALMOND MACAROONS -
Pareve

MAKES 3 DOZEN

- 6 oz. bittersweet chocolate
- 3/4 cup egg whites
  (4-5 large whites)
- 1/8 tsp. Passover cream of tartar
  or 1/8 tsp. lemon juice
- 3/4 cup sugar
- 1 egg yolk
- 1/2 cup ground blanched almonds
- 2 T cocoa powder

Preheat oven to 400° F. Grease 3 cookie sheets, dust with matzo cake meal, set aside.

Melt chocolate in top of double boiler, cool slightly. Beat egg whites and cream of tartar to soft peaks, gradually add sugar, add egg yolk. Reserve 2 T chocolate.

Fold 1/3 of beaten egg whites into chocolate mixture, fold in almonds and remaining egg whites. Use a pastry bag with plain 1/2" tip or two spoons to mound batter in rounds, one inch apart on cookie sheets. Bake one cookie sheet at a time 4 to 5 minutes until puffed. Cool 5 minutes. Spread bottoms of half the macaroons with chocolate, fit two together. Sift with cocoa before serving. Store airtight.

PERFECT PASSOVER POPOVERS - Pareve

From Barbara Fox, Buffalo, New York

MAKES 12 HUGE AIRY MUFFINS
FOR SANDWICHES

1/2 cup vegetable oil

1 cup water

1/4 tsp. salt

1/2 tsp. sugar

1 1/4 cup matzo meal
plus 1 T matzo meal

4 eggs, room temperature

Preheat oven to 400° F. Grease a 12 section muffin tin.

Boil oil, water and salt in a 2 qt. saucepan. Remove from heat, quickly and vigorously stir in matzo meal and sugar. Add whole eggs, one at a time, mixing each one thoroughly.

Fill prepared muffin tin three-fourths full. Bake 35 to 40 minutes. Cool. Store airtight. Use within two days.

Option: TO MAKE BAGELS: WITH MOISTENED HANDS, FORM 1" THICK ROPES OF DOUGH ABOUT 5 INCHES LONG, PINCH ENDS TOGETHER INTO A RING. ARRANGE BAGELS ON A GREASED COOKIE SHEET AND BAKE FOR 30 TO 40 MINUTES OR UNTIL BAGELS ARE GOLDEN. SERVE WARM.

PASSOVER BLINTZES - Pareve

MAKES ABOUT 16

3 eggs, room temperature

1 1/4 cup water

6 T potato starch

2 T matzo cake meal

1/2 tsp. salt

3 tsp. vegetable oil

Passover margarine **or** oil for frying

In a medium bowl, combine first five ingredients and mix well. Rest batter 30 minutes. Heat a 6" skillet on medium, brush it with melted margarine or vegetable oil. Place about 3 T batter in skillet and immediately rotate to evenly spread batter.

Cook until batter looks dry, flip blintz to other side. Cook 30 seconds. Invert skillet onto a clean kitchen towel. Continue making pancakes until all batter is used. Refrigerate or freeze separated by pieces of wax paper. Fill blintzes with cheese or fruit filling.

1 cup lowfat cottage cheese

2 to 3 T matzo meal

2 T sugar

1/2 T cinnamon

1 egg

oil **or** Passover margarine to fry

Cheese Filling

Combine all ingredients. Fill blintzes with 2T of cheese mixture. Keep filled blintzes chilled or frozen. Heat oil or margarine in large fry pan. Fry blintzes in batches. Serve immediately

PASSOVER CONFECTIONER'S SUGAR

1 cup super-fine granulated
sugar

2 tsp. potato starch

Process sugar until finely pulverized. Sift with potato starch; store airtight.

BASIC ICING - Pareve

1 cup prepared or purchased
Passover confectioner's sugar

1/2 cup Passover unsalted
margarine

2 T hot water

1/2 tsp. lemon juice

Combine confectioner's sugar and margarine in medium bowl, beat with electric mixer to combine. Add water a few drops at a time for the desired consistency. Add lemon juice. Spread with a metal spatula on a 9" cake layer.

Vary flavor with 2 T strong hot coffee instead of water; add 1 tsp. lemon zest; add 2 T orange juice and 1 tsp. orange zest or flavor with Passover jam.

MOCK WHIPPED CREAM - Dairy

1 cup skim milk

1 apple, peeled and finely
grated

3/4 cup sugar

1 egg white

grated rind of half a lemon

Process or blend all ingredients together for a long time, 10 minutes or more until close to the consistency of whipped cream. Frost cakes or garnish fruits and serve immediately. This does not hold up very long.

PASSOVER CANDY - Pareve

From Shirley Holub of Chicago

1 cup margarine

1 cup brown sugar

1 whole egg

1 cup cake meal

1 tsp. vanilla

1 package, 12 oz. mini
chocolate chips

Preheat oven to 350° F. Lightly grease a jellyroll pan.

In a medium bowl, with an electric hand mixer, cream together sugar and margarine. Mix in the egg, cake meal and vanilla.

Spread the mixture in the pan and bake 20 minutes. Remove pan from oven, spread with the chocolate chips. Return to oven and bake about 4 to 5 minutes until chips soften. Spread melted chocolate with a spatula. Chill to harden. Cut into squares. Store airtight.

MATZO - Pareve

3 cup unsifted, unbleached flour
1 cup water
dash of salt

Set the timer. Matzo can take only 18 minutes from the time water is added to the flour until it is taken from the oven. (Rabbis determined this time prevents leavening action.)

Preheat oven to 350° F. Mound flour on surface and slowly add water, kneading dough with hands until firm. Roll a handful of dough into a circle, using a long rolling pin. Prick lines of holes all over one side with a fork. Bake on an ungreased cookie sheet about 5 minutes, turn and bake 2 to 3 minutes more. Cool and store airtight.

Note: DO THIS WITH THE KIDS BEFORE PASSOVER. PROPER MATZO FLOUR IS USUALLY AVAILABLE COMMERCIALLY. "KOSHER L PESACH" MATZO IS MADE FROM FLOUR GUARDED FROM HARVEST THROUGH BAKING. IF A LOCAL BAKERY MAKES MATZO, ASK TO PURCHASE SOME FLOUR.

MANDLEN - Pareve

MAKES ABOUT 4 DOZEN
3 whole eggs **plus** 1 white
2 tsp. salt, fresh ground black pepper
1/2 cup matzo meal
1/4 cup potato starch
3/4 cup vegetable oil

Beat eggs and egg white with salt to just combine. Stir in matzo meal and potato starch. Grind in a few dashes of pepper. Heat oil in an 11" deep, heavy skillet to medium hot.

Using two teaspoons, scoop up ½" rounds of dough, drop in oil by the spoonful, don't crowd. Fry until evenly crisp, turn if necessary with a slotted spoon. Remove with slotted spoon, drain on paper towels. Serve hot or store in airtight container. Great in soup or salad.

MACAROON CRUST for PASSOVER - Pareve

3/4 cup crushed macaroons
2/3 cup chopped almonds
1/2 cup brown sugar
3 T matzo cake meal
1 T potato starch
1/4 tsp. salt
1/2 cup, (1 stick) unsalted Passover margarine, melted

Preheat oven to 350° F.

Process macaroons, almonds and brown sugar with matzo cake meal, potato starch and salt. With machine running, add melted margarine, mix 20 seconds. Pat into bottom and up sides of a 9" tart pan with removable sides. Bake 15 minutes. Touch sides of macaroon. If not set, bake 5 minutes more. Cool. Use a prepared filling. Garnish with additional macaroon crumbs.

CRUSTLESS APPLE PIE - Pareve

This recipe is adapted with the permission of Scribner, a Division of Simon & Schuster from *The Pie and Pastry Bible* by Rose Levy Beranbaum, Text Copyright © 1998 by Cordon Rose, Inc.

SERVES 8 TO 10

- 6 cups apple slices (about 4 large apples)
- 1 tsp. fresh lemon juice
- 2 T light brown sugar, packed
- 2 T granulated sugar
- 1/2 tsp. ground cinnamon
- 1/4 tsp. grated nutmeg
- 1/8 tsp. salt
- 1 T unsalted pareve Passover margarine

- 2 T vanilla sugar
- 1/2 cup walnuts, chopped
  dash of salt
- 1/2 tsp. ground cinnamon
- 4 T matzo cake meal
- 5 T unsalted pareve Passover margarine
- 3 T matzo meal

Preheat oven to 400° F. Set out a deep 9" pie plate.

In a large mixing bowl, combine apples, lemon juice, sugars, cinnamon, nutmeg and salt. Keep at room temperature about an hour. Toss occasionally.

Topping

For topping, process sugar, walnuts, salt and cinnamon until nuts are coarsely chopped. Add matzo cake meal and margarine, pulse until mixture is crumbly. Pour into a small bowl, add 1 T matzo meal and pinch mixture to assure mixture holds together in small clumps. Add remaining matzo meal if needed.

Spoon apples in a sieve placed over a clean bowl. Allow juices to drain; there should be about ¼ cup. In a small saucepan, heat the juice from the apples with 1 T margarine on medium-high heat. Simmer to reduce to 3 T.

Arrange apples in the pie pan and pour the reduced juice over the apples. Cover pan with foil, cut a steam vent in the foil and bake 35 minutes.

Remove the foil and spread the topping over the apples. Bake about 20 to 25 minutes longer. Topping will brown and apples will be tender when a sharp knife is inserted. Cool. Serve cut into wedges. (Pie keeps 3 days refrigerated.)

CORDON ROSE NEW YORK STYLE CHEESE CAKE - Dairy

This recipe is adapted with the permission of the author from *The Cake Bible* by Rose Levy Beranbaum, Text Copyright © 1988 by Cordon Rose, Inc., published by William Morrow & Co.

SERVES 16 OR MORE

- 1 lb. cream cheese (preferably Philadelphia)
- 1 cup sugar
- 2 tsp. potato starch
- 3 large eggs, room temperature
- 3 T fresh lemon juice
- 1½ tsp. Passover vanilla **or** vanilla sugar
- ¼ tsp. salt
- 3 cups sour cream

Preheat oven to 350° F. Grease sides and bottom of an 8 x 2½ inch springform pan; line with greased parchment. Wrap pan with a double layer of heavy-duty foil to prevent seepage.

In large bowl of electric mixer fitted with whisk beater, beat cream cheese and sugar until smooth. Add potato starch, eggs one at a time, beating well after each addition. Incorporate lemon juice, vanilla, salt and sour cream, beat until blended.

With a rubber scraper, scrape batter into pan. Set the cheesecake pan in a larger pan filled with 1" of hot water and bake 50 minutes. Turn oven off, do not open door for one hour. Remove cake to a rack and cool one hour. Cover with plastic and refrigerate overnight.

Line a flat plate with plastic wrap and have a serving dish ready. Place cake pan on a hot moist towel for 30 seconds. Run a thin spatula around sides of pan, release outer pan, turn onto plastic-lined plate. Remove bottom of pan and parchment. Re-invert onto serving dish, smooth sides with spatula. Chill until serving. Serve with berries if desired.

"AND YE SHALL OBSERVE THIS THING FOR AN ORDINANCE TO THEE AND TO THY

SON FOR EVER" —**EXODUS 12:24**

INDEX

cucumber and tomato salad, Middle East, 63
cucumber and tomatoes in yogurt, 65
cucumber soup, 27

D

date and nut bars, 151
desserts. *See* brownies; cakes; cookies; fruit
    desserts; mousse; pies; sorbet
dill sauce, 50
dried fruit compote, 144
drinks, strawberry banana smoothie, 12
drummettes and wings—polkes and
    fligels, 13

E

eggplant, and tomato soup with roasted
    peppers, 23
eggplant casserole, 39
eggplant moussaka, 113
eggplant slices, fried Sephardic, 53
eggplant spread, 56
eggs and salt water, 4
eggs, seven day Passover, 2
Egyptian charoset, 3
escalope of salmon and ginger, 85
European beef tsimmes, traditional, 101

F

farfel cookies, 150
fig and yogurt cheese pie, 137
fish
    bass, chilled sea, marinated in lemon and
        basil, 15
    carp, Becky's baked, 9
    fish chowder, 21

fish salad, 14
gefilte fish
    salmon steaks stuffed with, 7
    Spanish style, 8
    traditional, 6
    wrapped in cabbage leaves, 8
halibut wrapped in romaine, 10
salmon and ginger, escalope of, 85
salmon cakes with carmelized onions, 84
sardine dip, 10
snapper fillets with caper mayonnaise, 85
sweet and sour yellow pike, 9
flourless chocolate nut cake, 128
fried artichokes, Italian style, 49
frostings, meringue, 123
frozen lemon mousse, 119
fruit desserts
    apple nut ring, 145
    apple rhubarb crisp, 139
    apples with Israeli fruits and macaroons,
        baked, 146
    applesauce, 140
    citrus and berries, fresh, 140
    coconut macaroon cupcakes, 146
    dried fruit compote, 144
    melon compote with toasted almonds, 144
    orange slices with Moroccan spices, 141
    pear casserole, baked, 143
    pears, raspberry poached, 142
    pears, roasted in honey, 143
    pineapple slices, peppery fresh, 142
    strawberries in strawberries, 140
    strawberry rhubarb sauce, 145
    strawberry sauce, 141
fruit soup, Israeli, 29

G

garlic and almond soup, 26
garlic, roasted, 11
garlicky tomato salad, 61
gazpacho soup, chilled, 30

R

Other Fine Titles From
Five Star Publications, Incorporated

Most titles are available through
www.BarnesandNoble.com and www.amazon.com

Kosher Kettle: International Adventures in Jewish Cooking

By Sybil Ruth Kaplan, Foreword by Joan Nathan

With more than 350 recipes from 27 countries, this is one Kosher cookbook you don't want to be without. It includes everything from wheat halva from India to borrekas from Greece. Five Star Publications is donating a portion of all sales of *Kosher Kettle* to MAZON: A Jewish Response to Hunger. *A Jewish Book Club* selection.   ISBN 1-877749-19-2

That Hungarian's in My Kitchen

By Linda F. Radke

You won't want that Hungarian to leave your kitchen after you've tried some of the 125 Hungarian-American Kosher recipes that fill this delightful cookbook. Written for both the novice cook and the sophisticated chef, the cookbook comes complete with "Aunt Ethel's Helpful Hints."   ISBN 1-877749-28-1

Shoah: Journey From the Ashes

By Cantor Leo Fettman and Paul M. Howey

Cantor Leo Fettman survived the horrors of Auschwitz while millions of others, including almost his entire family, did not. He worked in the crematorium, was a victim of Dr. Josef Mengele's experiments, and lived through an attempted hanging by the SS. His remarkable tale of survival and subsequent joy is an inspiration for all. *Shoah* includes a historical prologue that chronicles the 2,000 years of anti-Semitism that led to the Holocaust. Cantor Fettman's message is one of love and hope, yet it contains an important warning for new generations to remember so the evils of the past will not be repeated.   ISBN 0-9679721-0-8

Shakespeare: To Teach or Not to Teach

By Cass Foster and Lynn G. Johnson

The answer is a resounding "To Teach!" There's nothing dull about this guide for anyone teaching Shakespeare in the classroom, with activities such as crossword puzzles, a scavenger hunt, warm-up games, and costume and scenery suggestions.   ISBN 1-877749-03-6

Shakespeare for Children: The Story of Romeo and Juliet

By Cass Foster

Adults shouldn't keep a classic this good to themselves. This fully illustrated book makes the play easily understandable to young readers, yet it is faithful to the spirit of the original. A *Benjamin Franklin Children's Storybooks Award* nominee.   ISBN 0-9619853-3-x

The Sixty-Minute Shakespeare Series

By Cass Foster

Not enough time to tackle the unabridged versions of the world's most widely read playwright? Pick up a copy of *Romeo and Juliet* (ISBN 1-877749-38-9), *A Midsummer Night's Dream* (ISBN 1-877749-37-0), *Hamlet* (ISBN 1-87749-40-0), *Macbeth* (ISBN 1-877749-41-9), *Much Ado About Nothing* (ISBN 1-877749-42-7), and *Twelfth Night* (ISBN 1-877749-39-7) and discover how much more accessible Shakespeare can be to you and your students.

The Adventures of Andi O'Malley

By Celeste Messer

(1)   Angel Experiment JR134

Ashley Layne is the richest and most popular girl in school. In an unusual twist, Andi is given the opportunity to know what it's truly like to be Ashley Layne. Travel with Andi as she discovers that things are not always as they seem. ISBN 0-9702171-0-2

(2) The Broken Wing

Andi is visited by a little angel who needs her help in more ways than one. The angel has broken her wing in a midair collision with another, larger angel and desperately needs Andi to hide her while she heals. Rather than hide her, Andi takes the little angel to school with her where no one could have expected the lessons they would learn!   ISBN 0-9702171-1-0

(3) The Gift

Andi receives an assignment from her guardian angel. At first, she's excited, but she becomes furious when she realizes what the job involves. Although Andi tries desperately to get out of completing her assignment, she learns there is no turning back. What happens in the end could only happen to Andi O'Malley!
ISBN 0-9702171-3-7

(4) The Circle of Light

The world is about to be taken over by Zykien, the most evil of all angels of darkness. With the help of the rather odd-looking Miss Bluebonnet, Andi and her friends discover the incredible power of goodness that can result when people work together. Even the Tashonians, the tiniest of creatures, play an important role in restoring peace and love to the world.
ISBN 0-9702171-2-9

(5) Three Miracles

Three young people are in a terrible accident caused by a drunk driver. Their voices are heard—but only by Andi's friend Troy. When he proves to Andi and her sister and brother that he's not making it up, the three voices give them three tasks that will change their lives and the lives of several others forever.   ISBN 0-9702171-4-5

The Proper Pig's Guide to Mealtime Manners

By L.A. Kowal and Sally Starbuck Stamp
No one in your family would ever act like a pig at mealtime, but perhaps you know another family with that problem. This whimsical guide, complete with its own ceramic pig, gives valuable advice for children and adults alike on how to make mealtimes more fun and mannerly.   ISBN 1-877749-20-6

The Economical Guide to Self-Publishing: How to Produce and Market Your Book on a Budget

By Linda F. Radke
This book is a must-have for anyone who is or wants to be a self-publisher. It is a valuable step-by-step guide for producing and promoting your book effectively, even on a limited budget. The book is filled with tips on avoiding common, costly mistakes and provides resources that can save you lots of money—not to mention headaches. A *Writer's Digest Book Club* selection.
ISBN 1-877749-16-8

Linda F. Radke's Promote Like a Pro: Small Budget, Big Show

By Linda F. Radke
In this step-by-step guide, self-publishers can learn how to use the print and broadcast media, public relations, the Internet, public speaking, and other tools to market books—without breaking the bank! In *Linda Radke's Promote Like a Pro: Small Budget, Big Show*, a successful publisher and a group of insiders offer self-publishers valuable information about promoting books.   ISBN 1-87749-36-2

Letters of Love: Stories from the Heart

Edited by Salvatore Caputo
In this warm collection of love letters and stories, a group of everyday people share hopes, dreams, and experiences of love: love won, love lost, and love found again. Most of all, they share their belief that love is a blessing that makes life's challenges worthwhile.
ISBN 1-877749-35-4

Nannies, Maids & More: The Complete Guide for Hiring Household Help

By Linda F. Radke

Anyone who has had to hire household help knows what a challenge it can be. This book provides a step-by-step guide to hiring—and keeping—household help, complete with sample ads, interview questions, and employment forms.   ISBN 0-9619853-2-1

Household Careers: Nannies, Butlers, Maids & More: The Complete Guide for Finding Household Employment

By Linda F. Radke

Numerous professional positions are available in the child-care and home-help fields. This award-winning book provides all the information you need to find and secure a household job.   ISBN 1-877749-05-2

Tying the Knot: The Sharp Dresser's Guide to Ties and Handkerchiefs

By Andrew G. Cochran

This handy little guide contains everything you want (or need) to know about neckties, bow ties, pocket squares, and handkerchiefs—from coordinating ties and shirts to tying a variety of knots.   ISBN 0-9630152-6-5

For the Record: A Personal Facts and Document Organizer

By Ricki Sue Pagano

Many people have trouble keeping track of the important documents and details of their lives. Ricki Sue Pagano designed *For the Record* so they could regain control—and peace of mind. This organizing tool helps people keep track and makes it easy to find important documents in a pinch.   ISBN 0-9670226-0-6

Junk Mail Solution

By Jackie Plusch

Jackie Plusch's Junk Mail Solution can help stop the aggravating intrusion of unwanted solicitations by both mail and phone. She offers three easy steps for freeing yourself from junk mailers and telemarketers. The book also includes pre-addressed cards to major mass marketing companies and handy script cards to put by your phones.   ISBN 0-9673136-1-9